This item must be returned on or before
the date stamped below.

1 5 JAN 2014		

P

i

P

th

Sa

facet publishing

© CILIP: the Chartered Institute of Library and Information Professionals, 2004

Published by
Facet Publishing
7 Ridgmount Street
London WC1E 7AE

Facet Publishing (formerly Library Association Publishing) is wholly owned by CILIP: the Chartered Institute of Library and Information Professionals.

Sandy Norman has asserted her right under the Copyright Designs and Patents Act 1988, to be identified as the author of this work.

First published 2004

British Library Cataloguing in Publication Data
A catalogue record for this book is available from the British Library.

ISBN 1-85604-490-4

Disclaimer

While every care has been taken in compiling this work to reflect and give expression to the law, the author and CILIP cannot claim that it is a definitive work nor that it constitutes legal advice, and therefore they will not accept any liability for any damage caused by reliance on any advice given. If in doubt, it is advisable to err on the side of caution and, where necessary, to seek appropriate legal advice.

Typeset in 11/13pt Elegant Garamond and Dax by Facet Publishing.
Printed and made in Great Britain by MPG Books Ltd, Bodmin, Cornwall.

Contents

Preface

My main aims in producing this guide are to promote respect and understanding of copyright and related rights, and to help those who work in the library and information sector to continue to provide a satisfactory service to their clientele while continuing to remain on the right side of the law. Although this work is intended primarily for those working in the information sector, it can also be a useful source of copyright information and guidance on copyright and licensing issues for anyone who is faced with a copyright issue. I hope also that by reading this book, many may come to find copyright as interesting as I have over the years.

This work is an updated successor to my previously published sectoral copyright guides for librarians. Although it contains a lot more detail than the previous versions, this publication is not intended to be a comprehensive legal textbook on the law of copyright, but simply a practical handbook and companion to the many people in the library and information profession who for various reasons want to understand and comply with copyright law. It is intended to be read by those having limited or even no knowledge of copyright and related rights and who wish to learn more, and for those who deal with copyright issues on a regular basis and who wish to keep themselves up to date. Many readers will have enough knowledge just to dip in and out when necessary. For those of you who are new to the law of copyright, my advice follows the recommended practice of how to eat an elephant – in easy bite-sized chunks. I have summarized ten useful points at the end of each chapter to help make digestion easier.

Copyright is a difficult subject to understand – a minefield, as so many of you have said to me over the years. So, I have tried to explain as simply as possible the intricacies of the Copyright, Designs and Patents Act 1988, hereafter referred to as 'the Act', and its effects on information professionals and users of information, while adding some common-sense guidance on compliance on the way. Although it can be dangerous, so the experts say, to impart only a little knowledge, the complexities of copyright in all its glorious detail and legal jargon are enough to turn readers off completely, so I have attempted to provide enough information on a need-to-know basis without going into too much legal detail. Experience, positive feedback and evaluation of how I work assure me that this kind of guide or handbook will be just enough.

The current Act took effect from August 1989 and applies throughout the UK. There have been several amendments since then following from the EU harmonization programme. The latest amendments, which came into force on

31 October 2003, implement the EU Copyright Directive obligations. These Copyright and Related Rights Regulations 2003 also include new sections on copying by visually impaired persons, which were introduced by the enactment of the Copyright (Visually Impaired Persons) Act 2002, and the new responsibilities for ISPs contained in the Electronic Commerce (EC Directive) Regulations 2002. This work contains all the relevant changes, a list of which is given below.

Extracts from the text of the Act and relevant Statutory Instruments have been included where relevant. References are made to relevant numbered sections, and it is recommended that these be consulted when more detail is required.

It should be borne in mind that the law, agreements with rights holders and licensing schemes are all subject to change. Any changes will be reported in the *CILIP Update* and other professional journals, and on the Libraries and Archives Copyright Alliance (LACA) website (see Chapter 10, pages 164–5).

The Copyright and Related Rights Regulations 2003: relevant changes

- communication to the public right replacing 'broadcasting and inclusion in a cable programme service'
- a new definition of broadcast to establish the difference between a static and an interactive transmission
- minor changes to the duration of a sound recording
- inclusion of an exception for making transient or incidental copies
- a ban on copying for research for a commercial purpose with subsequent changes to fair dealing and the library exceptions
- a new definition of private study to exclude any study which is directly or indirectly for a commercial purpose
- a definition of 'made available to the public'
- a requirement to acknowledge all works copied under an exception unless impractical
- a ban on any commercial copying in education
- changes to the exceptions for playing sound recordings in clubs or societies, time shifting, making a photograph from a broadcast, and playing a broadcast in public
- changes to copying unpublished works if author dead for more than 70 years
- injunctions against service providers
- new rights given to make circumvention of technical protection systems and rights management systems illegal
- new rules for copying for visually impaired people implemented as a result of the Copyright (Visually Impaired Persons Act) 2003.

Acknowledgements

I wish to thank my friends and colleagues at LACA and CILIP for their support and encouragement over the years; colleagues at EBLIDA for their help in lobbying for balanced copyright laws in Europe; colleagues at IFLA CLM for advising me on national differences; and all those personal members of CILIP, those who I have met on my copyright training courses, plus all those information professionals across all sectors who have provided me with plenty of topics, questions and inspiration in writing this work.

I am indebted to Denise Nicholson of the University of Witwatersrand for the information in the report on South Africa and to Bob Oakley, Director of the Law Library and Professor of Law, Georgetown University Law Library, for giving me information about happenings in the USA. I gratefully acknowledge the permission given by Avril Ward of the Learning and Skills Council to include the suggested permission-seeking text (see Fig. 5.1, page 73) from its in-house guide; by Charles Oppenheim, to use some of his examples of what is and is not commercial research (see Fig 4.1, page 48); and by IFLA, to quote from its copyright position papers. I would also like to thank the CLA and NLA for providing me with full information about their licensing schemes.

Above all I would like to thank Len for being patient and understanding, and for providing tea and sustenance.

Sandy Norman

1 Copyright basics

In this chapter you will learn about:

- the nature of copyright
- the economic and moral rights an author is able to exploit and control
- definitions of works protected
- who owns copyright
- the different terms of protection
- other intellectual property rights, including database right and publication right.

What is copyright?

Copyright is a member of the family of intellectual property (IP) rights. Other IP rights include designs, patents, trademarks and database right, a fairly recent introduction into UK law. Details of these are given at the end of this chapter. IP rights give protection to businesses wishing to exploit them and are intended to complement each other, although they each stand alone.

Copyright exists to protect the works of authors and performers for a specified period of time during which they are able to exploit their works in any way they wish. Copyright is a property right and may be traded like any other commodity. Once a work has met the criteria for protection, authors (creators) are automatically given a bundle of rights to manage and exploit. These are called the economic rights and may be bought and sold like property or be assigned or licensed for a specified period.

Exploitation of a work means that an author is given the opportunity to profit from selling, assigning or licensing their economic rights. However, not all authors see that as the main reason for creating. Many authors, e.g. academic authors and those sharing works and images on the web, may wish to waive their rights because they do not want to make money out of their works. However, it is fair to say that all authors would expect their works to be acknowledged.

Economic rights

The various economic rights are given below, with reference to the relevant sections of the Copyright, Designs and Patents Act 1988 and appropriate Statutory Instrument.

The reproduction right (s. 17)

Copying – the right to copy the work – means reproducing a work in any material form, and includes the storing of a work in any medium by electronic means and the making of a copy which is transient or incidental to some other use of the work.

With regard to artistic works, it is also a restricted act to make a copy in three dimensions of a two-dimensional work and make a copy in two dimensions of a three-dimensional work. For example, it is not allowed to construct a building from an architect's drawing without permission, and it is not allowed to take a photograph of a sculpture without permission. However, there is an exception for this in section 62 (see Chapter 2, page 36).

The right to publish (s. 18)

This is the right to issue copies of the work to the public. It is the act of putting into circulation copies not previously put into circulation by or with the consent of the copyright owner and any subsequent distribution, sale, hiring or loan of copies, i.e. rental and lending.

Rental and lending rights (s. 18A and SI 1996 No. 2967)

These are rights to control the hiring or lending of a work or copy of the work to the public. More details on this are given in Chapter 3.

Performance rights (s. 19)

These are rights to perform, show or play the work in public A performance includes delivery of a lecture, speech or sermon as well as a visual or acoustic presentation using a sound recording, film or broadcast.

Communication to the public right (s. 20)

This is the new right to communicate a literary, dramatic, musical or artistic work, or a sound recording, film or broadcast, to the public by electronic transmission. This right covers broadcasting of works as well as making them available to the public in such a way that members of the public may access the work at a time and from a place convenient to them, e.g. on the internet.

Adaptation right (ss. 16–21)

Adaptation right is the right to make an adaptation of a work or do any of the above in relation to the adaptation. This usually means adapting a literary, dramatic or musical work into a different format, e.g. from a novel into a play, or it could mean making a translation from one language to another. It also applies to altering or changing the arrangement of computer programs or databases. Adaptation right does not apply to artistic works, so one artist may imitate the style of another without infringing copyright. However, in the process no copying of the other artist's work should take place.

Moral rights

Moral rights belong to authors and are independent of the economic rights of copyright. It is important to be aware of them as they become increasingly relevant in the digital environment.

The right of paternity (s. 77–79)

This is the right of the author to be identified as such when their works are commercially published, performed or communicated to the public. This right has to be asserted. Examples can be seen on the title-page verso of many publications and on the backs of photographs or the mounts of transparencies or slides. There are exceptions to paternity right, e.g. it does not apply to computer programs, design of typefaces and computer-generated works, and also does not apply to works generated in the course of employment.

The right of integrity (s. 80)

This is the right of the author to prevent or object to derogatory treatment of their work. Treatment is defined to mean an addition to, deletion from or alteration to or adaptation of the work. (Adaptation in this sense does not apply to a translation of a literary, dramatic or musical work.) The treatment of a work would be seen as derogatory if it is distorted or mutilated or is otherwise seen as being prejudicial to the honour or reputation of the author. This is extremely relevant for works in digital format, especially artistic works, which can be easily manipulated. However, as this moral right was introduced in the 1988 Act it does not, strictly speaking, apply to works created before then.

False attribution (s. 84)

This is the right of persons not to have a literary, dramatic, musical or artistic work falsely attributed to them.

The right of disclosure (s. 85)

This is the right of the author to withhold certain photographs or films from publication. Under the UK Act this would apply to a person who commissions the work but decides not to have it issued to the public, exhibited or shown in public, or included in a broadcast.

Obtaining copyright protection

There is no legal requirement to register copyright in order to obtain it. Copyright protection is automatic and there is no other formality. For a literary, dramatic or musical work to qualify it must however be *original*, i.e. not a facsimile copy of another work, and it has to be expressed in a recognizable form, i.e. recorded in some way (written down, painted, composed, etc.).

A sound recording or film only qualifies if it has not been taken from another sound recording or film. Such a work may still be protected even if the work is recorded without the permission of the author, so a bootleg recording of a performance is still protected by copyright.

The use of the copyright symbol – © – is not necessary in order to obtain copyright. The © symbol is commonly used in published written works to draw the readers attention to the holder of the rights in a work and the conditions of use. It is good practice to use the copyright symbol to indicate who owns the copyright and the year the work was created.

Any author concerned that their work may be misappropriated before publication may take precautions by depositing the work with their bank, or they could put the unpublished work in an envelope, seal and date it and post it to themselves, and then if there is a dispute the unopened envelope could be proof of first authorship.

Works protected by copyright and related rights and their definitions

Copyright protects original literary, dramatic, musical and artistic works, sound recordings, films (and videos), broadcasts (including cable and satellite broadcasts) and the typographical arrangements of published editions of a literary, dramatic or musical work. It makes no difference whether these works are in print (published or unpublished) or electronic format, so letters, e-mail messages, works included in an electronic database (CD-ROMs) and material on websites are protected too.

Literary, dramatic and musical works (s. 3)

These are works which are written, spoken or sung, including a table or compilation, a computer program with preparatory design material for computer programs, or a database. A dramatic work includes a work of dance or mime, and a musical work means a work consisting of music. This is exclusive of any words or action intended to be sung, spoken or performed with the music, these being separate copyrights.

Databases (s. 3A)

Databases are protected as literary works, but only if they fulfil the criteria for protection. Full copyright protection is given to those databases which by virtue of their selection and arrangement of the contents constitute the author's own intellectual creation. (If a database does not fulfil the criteria for protection it may be protected by database right – see below). The definition given of a database is very broad and includes any structured collection, whether in print or electronic format, of works, data or other material arranged in a systematic or methodical way and individually accessible by electronic or other means. Collections of data include directories, encyclopaedias, yearbooks, statistical databases, online collections of journals, multimedia collections. Web pages and other collections of data on the internet could also be covered. (It may also be that newspapers or learned journals are caught in the definition, but until this has been established by case law it is advisable to treat them as journals and periodicals.)

Database right (SI 1997 No. 3032)

The criterion for qualification for database right is that a substantial investment must have been made in the obtaining, verification and presentation of its contents by the database maker. So, although a database must be original to qualify for copyright, it need not be original to qualify for database right. All this is regardless of the actual *contents*, which may or may not have copyright protection in their own right.

Artistic works (s. 4)

An artistic work is defined as including graphic works, photographs, sculptures or collages. This is irrespective of artistic quality. For example, holiday snaps may not contain any artistic merit but they are nevertheless protected. Also included under this definition are works of architecture, i.e. buildings or a model for a building, and works of artistic craftsmanship. A library building is therefore protected by copyright.

A graphic work includes any painting, drawing, diagram, map, chart or plan, and any engraving, etching, lithograph, woodcut or similar work. Plans of a library are therefore covered by this definition.

A photograph is defined as a recording of light or other radiation on any medium on which an image is produced or from which an image may by any means be produced, and which is not part of a film, and a sculpture includes a cast or model made for purposes of sculpture.

Typographical arrangement of published editions (s. 8)

This means the way the words are arranged on the pages of books and other literary materials. It is a separate copyright from the author's copyright and it only applies if the arrangement is original, i.e. it is not a facsimile reproduction of a previous edition.

Sound recordings (s. 5A)

Sound recordings are defined as recordings of sounds, from which the sounds may be reproduced, or recordings of the whole or any part of a literary, dramatic or musical work, from which sounds reproducing the work or part of the work may be produced, regardless of the medium on which the recording is made or the method by which the sounds are reproduced or produced. This means that the format of the recording makes no difference to whether the work is protected or not. There is no new copyright in a sound recording if it is a copy taken from a previous sound recording.

Films (s. 5B)

A film 'means a recording on any medium from which a moving image may by any means be produced.' The soundtrack accompanying a film is treated as part of the film under this definition, although the film soundtrack is a separate copyright. The Act says also that 'copyright does not subsist in a film which is, or to the extent that it is, a copy taken from a previous film'. It is interesting to note that before 1957, films were not protected by copyright as such, although the individual frames were protected as photographs. Fiction films before that date qualified as dramatic works.

Broadcasts (s. 6)

Since the implementation of the Copyright and Related Rights Regulations 2003, the definition of a broadcast has been redefined. The legislators have tried to make it absolutely clear that a broadcast is different from static internet web pages or on-demand transmissions whereby a person can call up a programme when they like, e.g. on the BBC website where radio listeners may hear programme repeats when they like. A broadcast has been defined to mean 'an electronic transmission of visual images, sounds or other information' which is 'transmitted for simultaneous reception by members of the public' and which 'is capable of being lawfully received by them'. It can also be an electronic transmission which 'is transmitted at a time determined solely by the person making the transmission for presentation to members of the public'.

Some material on the internet could be defined as a broadcast if it is transmitted live. A webcast or a simulcast is a broadcast.

What is not protected by copyright

Copyright does not protect individual bibliographic citations, facts and headlines, although a collection of them would be protected by copyright and/or database right. After the copyright in a work has expired (see below for the various copyright terms) it is considered to be in the public domain and may be used freely.

Some countries, for instance the USA, do not protect legislative or statutory material created by government servants.

The first owners of copyright (ss. 9–11)

The first owner of copyright in a literary, dramatic, musical or artistic work is the person who creates it, who is usually called the author. If a creator wishes to exploit any of their rights, this is usually by an assignment in writing. Creators may also bequeath copyright on death to their heirs or successors.

For *sound recordings*, the owner is the person who puts the recording together, i.e. the producer.

For *films*, the copyright owner is the producer and the principal director, unless they are same person. From 1 June 1957 until 30 June 1994, the first owner was the producer. The first owners of any fiction films produced before 1 June 1957 could be the owner of the negatives of each of the frames and/or the author of the dramatic work.

The person making a *broadcast* owns the copyright in what is broadcast.

The *typographical arrangement* of a published edition copyright is owned by the publisher.

If a literary, dramatic, musical or artistic work is *computer-generated*, the author is the 'person by whom the arrangements necessary for the creation of the work are undertaken'.

For *databases* the first owner is the 'person who takes the initiative in obtaining, verifying or presenting the contents of a database and assumes the risk of investing in that obtaining, verification or presentation' (SI 1997 No. 3032). This person is called the database maker. If the database maker is an employee, the employer is regarded as the database maker subject to any agreement to the contrary. So the employer will own the library catalogue, for example.

Since August 1989 the first owner of a *photograph* has been the photographer. However, if the photograph was taken any time between 1 July 1912 and 1 August 1989, the first owner was normally the person who held the material on which it was made, e.g. the negatives. This could be the photographer or the person who commissioned the photograph.

The Queen owns *Crown copyright*, defined in section 163 of the Act as covering those works 'made by Her Majesty or by an officer or servant of the Crown in the course of his duties'. The Crown may also own other material not originally produced by Crown servants if copyright has been assigned or transferred to the Crown by the legal owner of the rights. The responsibility for the management and licensing of copyrights owned by the Crown rests with the Controller of HMSO in her capacity as Queen's Printer and Queen's Printer for Scotland.

The legal copyright holders of *Parliamentary copyright* are the Speaker of the House of Commons, in respect of Commons material, and the Clerk of the Parliaments, in respect of Lords material. Parliamentary copyright covers any work made by or under the direction of the House of Commons or the House of Lords (s. 165). It covers works published by Parliament since the Act took effect on 1 August 1989. Before this date all published material produced by Parliament was covered by Crown copyright.

Works created under the terms of an employment contract

If a work is created as part of the terms of employment, the law assumes that the employer will own copyright unless there is a contract to the contrary. This is important to remember, as the law will assume that copyright in material created by employees of any organization will be owned by the organization. Note that this does not apply to works generated by the Crown, Parliament or some international organizations. Some institutions have chosen to distinguish in contracts of employment between material created directly for teaching, i.e. course documentation, and scholarly activity such as journal articles or books. There is much variation among HE institutions in this respect.

The length of the copyright term

Copyright protection is not designed to be perpetual, so at some time a work will cease to be protected. When a work does go out of copyright it is said to fall into the public domain, which means it is available for anyone to copy and use. However, copyright protection is designed to give authors and their heirs the opportunity to fully exploit a work if they so wish, so a work may not fall into the public domain for many years. Each material is treated differently. Not all copyright terms are the same.

Literary, dramatic, musical and artistic works (s. 12)

For a literary, dramatic, musical or artistic work, copyright normally expires 70 years after the end of the year of a known author's death. Literary works includes databases which fulfil the criteria for selection. However, for works of unknown authorship, expiry is 70 years from the end of the calendar year in which the work was made, or 70 years from when the work was first legally made available to the public. *Made available to the public* with respect to a literary, dramatic or musical work includes performance in public or communication to the public. For an artistic work, it includes being exhibited in public, included in a film being shown to the public or communicated to the public.

Unknown authorship

If the author of the work in question is unknown, copyright expires 70 years after the end of the calendar year in which the work was made, or, if it was made available to the public during that period, 70 years after the end of the calendar year in which the work was first made available. This applies to all works of unknown authorship except some photographs.

Joint authorship

For works of joint authorship, the copyright expires 70 years following the last known person to die.

Non-EEA works

Although under Berne and the UCC (see Chapter 8, pages 138–40) one of the main principles is national treatment – protecting foreign works in the same way as national works, and treating them in the same way – it is important to note that this does not apply if the term of protection in the home nation is greater than that of the foreign nation. For example: the European Economic Area term of protection does not apply to non-EEA states. For works published in countries outside the EEA, the duration of copyright entitlement is according to the law of that country, provided it does not exceed that of the EEA. For example, if the work in question comes from a country where copyright expires (according to the Berne minimum) 50 years after the end of the year of the death of the author, then the copyright in the work would be considered to have expired 50 years after the calendar year it was made or legally made available to the public. This ruling applies to all protected works.

Unpublished works

In the 1988 Act, unpublished manuscripts were given copyright only until 50 years from the death of the author, not in perpetuity (or until publication) as in previous legislation. However, that material already in copyright when the Act came into force (i.e. works by an author who died before August 1989) remained in copyright until the end of 2039 (Sch. 1, s. 12(4)). When the EU regulations which extended the term of copyright protection were introduced, the basic rule was that anyone who qualified had their work protected for life plus 70 years. Copyright should not last any longer than life plus 70 years nor should copyright protection be reduced. Therefore the unpublished works of authors who died well before 1969 would still be protected only until the end of 2039, and those authors who died after 1969 will have their works protected for life plus 70 years. So if an author is known, but their work remains unpublished, copyright lasts for the standard term of author's life plus 70 years, apart from those who died before 1969.

Photographs

The term of protection for photographs can be very confusing. Calculating the copyright term for photographs depends on several things:

- whether the author is known or unknown
- when the photograph was taken
- whether the photograph has been published or unpublished
- whether the photograph is subject to Crown, Parliamentary or international organization copyright.

If the author of the photograph is known, the normal standard term for all literary, dramatic, musical or artistic works applies, i.e. copyright expires 70 years after the end of the calendar year of the photographer's death. However, there are some exceptions which need to be taken into account. Bear in mind also that the first owner may not always be the photographer.

If the author of the photograph is known *and* the photograph was taken before 1 June 1957, copyright expires 70 years after the death of the author.

If the author of the photograph is known *and* if the work was created on or after 1 June 1957 and before 1 August 1989 *and* the author died before 1 January 1969 *and* the work had never been published or at least had not been published before 1 August 1989, copyright will expire on 31 December 2039.

If the author of the photograph is known *and* the photograph was created on or after 1 June 1957 and was published before 1 August 1989 and the author died more than 20 years before publication, copyright will expire 50 years after the end of the year of first publication.

If the author of the photograph is known and the photograph was created on or after 1 June 1957 *and* was published before 1 August 1989 *and* the author died less than 20 years before publication, copyright will expire 70 years after the end of the year of the author's death.

If the author of the photograph is unknown, expiration of copyright depends on when the work was first made or made available to the public (see above for details). If the year is known, then copyright expires 70 years following the end of that year.

If the author of the photograph is unknown *and* the work was created on or after 1 June 1957 and before 1 January 1969 *and* it was not published before 1 August 1989 *and* it was not made available to the public before 1 January 2040, then copyright will expire on 31 December 2039.

If Crown copyright applies, protection is for a maximum of 125 calendar years unless published commercially, in which case a photograph is protected for only 50 calendar years from the end of the year in which it was created. Photographs subject to Parliamentary copyright are protected for 50 calendar years from taking. Photographs whose copyright belongs to any of the international organizations are protected for 50 calendar years from the end of the year in which the photograph was taken.

Sound recordings (s. 13A)

The term of protection for a sound recording is 50 years from the end of the year in which the recording was made, or if during that period the recording is released, 50 years from the end of the calendar year in which it was first released. However, if the recording is not released during that period but is made available to the public, the term is 50 years from being made available. 'Made available to the public' is defined here as being played in public or communicated to the public. However, a sound recording would not be considered to be published if it was first played on the internet without authorization.

Films (s. 13B)

Copyright expires 70 years after the death of the last to die of the following: the principal director, the author of the screenplay, the author of the dialogue or the composer of the music created for and used in the film, subject to a few provisions.

Broadcasts (s. 14)

Copyright expires at the end of the period of 50 years from the end of the calendar year in which the broadcast was made.

Typographical arrangement (s. 15)

The typographical arrangement copyright is 25 years from the end of the year of publication. So, if a work by an author who died over 70 years ago is brought out in a new edition with an original typographical arrangement, then the work will attract a new term of protection for 25 years from the date of publication. This is important to remember. One can never assume that a work is truly out of copyright unless the edition is over 25 years old and the author has been dead for over 70 years. Bear in mind also that there may be other copyrights to consider: a foreword or introduction which is added to any new edition. These of course attract the full copyright term for their authors.

Publication right

The term for publication right (see page 13) lasts for 25 years from the year a work is first published, and has protection in the same way as other newly created works and is subject to the same provisions. Sound recordings do not attract publication right and the right does not apply to expired Crown or Parliamentary copyright material.

Crown and Parliamentary copyright, and copyright in certain international organizations

Crown copyright lasts for 125 years from production (s. 163). However, copyright in published material produced by the Crown lasts for 50 years from the date of publication. To give an example, text created by a government employee is protected for 125 years from the date of creation as it is Crown copyright. If the text is published within a few months of creation, the published work has a protection for 50 years from the date of publication. If the work is not published until 25, 50 or even 75 years later, the work will still only have a 50-year protection.

Parliamentary copyright in a literary, dramatic, musical or artistic work subsists for 50 years from the end of the year in which it was made (s. 165).

Copyright in works produced by certain international organizations, where they are the first owners, subsists for 50 years from the end of the year in which they were made (s. 168).

Database right

The basic term of protection for database right against unfair extraction and reutilization of the contents is for 15 years after the end of the calendar year in which the database was made. However, any substantial change to the database during this time (additions, deletions or alterations) which results in additional substantial investment gives rise to a further 15-year extension. Just how extensive these changes have to be before the database deserves a further term is not known. It is likely that many dynamic databases will be protected indefinitely.

Other IP rights

Publication right

In Council Directive No. 93/98/EEC (the Duration Directive) a new right was given to literary, dramatic, musical, artistic works or films in which copyright has expired and which have not previously been published. Called publication right, this was implemented into the UK Act as part of the Copyright and Related Rights Regulations 1996 (SI 1996 No. 2967). The definition of publication is very broad and includes making available to the public, in particular: issuing copies to the public, making the work available by an electronic retrieval system; rental and lending to the public; performing, exhibiting or showing the work in public; or communicating the work to the public. In order to publish a work, a publisher must be authorized to do so. Permission must be obtained from the owner of the 'physical medium on which the work is embodied'. Works which are published without authorization would not qualify for this right, and in order for publishers to qualify for this right they must be an EEA national at the time of publication and the work must be first published in an EEA state.

This right will have little effect on libraries and archives, as most unpublished material will still be in copyright until 2039 at least. Also, most copyright-expired material in libraries would already have been made available to the public and therefore technically published. Therefore, the only materials which are likely to be affected are very old works. Some very old photographs and other documents in local studies collections which are not on open inspection (over 150 years old at least) may fall into these categories. However, the third hurdle is that potential publishers are obliged to ask the owner (or keeper) for permission to use their material. This could be refused if felt necessary. Also, there could be a problem if publication right was asserted erroneously, as there do not appear to be any sanctions for false assertion.

Database right

Databases are a special case, as authors are given a new form of property protection if they meet the necessary criteria. Database owners have the right to prevent unfair extraction and reutilization of their contents. Full copyright protection is still given to those databases which are original in the selection and arrangement of their contents, but a compilation which does not meet the originality criteria for copyright protection is able to be protected by database right.

Trademarks

A trademark is any sign that can distinguish the goods and services of one trader from the goods or services of another. Such signs are usually graphical and can include words (e.g. personal names), designs, letters, slogans and the shape of goods or their packaging, but a trademark could also be a sound, a shape or even a smell. A trademark is used as a marketing tool so that customers can recognize the product of a particular trader.

There are two types of trademarks: registered and unregistered. The symbol of an unregistered trademark is ™ whereas the symbol of a registered trademark is ®. If marks are registered they confer greater rights on their owners. Registered trademarks are subject to approval and payment, and can be in force indefinitely. The initial registration is for ten years and this may continually be renewed for another ten. If, however, a mark is proved not to have been used for five years, registration may be revoked. Generally the problem with trademarks is where one trader infringes their use by passing another's trademark off as their own. Trademark owners have the remedy of suing for infringement of registered marks, or if the trademark is not registered they may bring a common law action for passing off. Although the trademark could have copyright as an artistic work, for copying for the purposes of research, private study or educational purposes, CILIP believes that trademark owners are unlikely to bring an action of copyright infringement.

Patents

Patents protect inventions and give a right to the inventor to prevent others from making, using or selling the invention for up to 20 years. To qualify for this right, the invention must be novel (never been made public before), involve an inventive step (different from a previous version or work) and be capable of industrial application. Patents have to be applied for and are subject to payment.

Designs

Like trademarks, there are two types of designs: registered and unregistered. Unregistered design is an automatic right given to creators of the design. This right lasts for a maximum of 15 years. Anyone is entitled to obtain a licence to exploit the design within the last five years. Design right only applies if and when the design is recorded in a design document or an article made to the design.

If required, designs may be registered at the Patent Office. Information on designs and registration may be found on their website. A registered design is a monopoly right for the appearance of the whole or a part of a product resulting from the features of, in particular, the lines, contours, colours, shape, texture or materials of the product or its implementation. Registration is for an initial period of 5 years but this may be renewed every 5 years up to a maximum of 25 years. A registered design is additional to any design right or copyright protection that may exist automatically in the design.

There is an organization which acts as a design-infringement watchdog called ACID (Anti Copying in Design). This organization may be applied to regarding copying product designs. ACID also deals with logos, furniture and fashion.

Ten things to remember from this chapter

- copyright is automatic: there is no need to register it
- the © copyright symbol is not necessary in order to obtain copyright
- copyright is a property right; rights may be bought and sold
- the standard term of protection for copyright is life plus 70 years
- unpublished works remain in copyright until at least 2039
- there are different terms of protection for different materials
- the term of protection for a photograph depends on whether the author is known or not, whether it is published or not, when it was made and who by
- publishers have a 25-year copyright on their published works, so even if an author is out of copyright, their works may still be protected
- an employer normally owns copyright in works created by employees
- databases that qualify for protection are protected by copyright and/or database right.

2 Exceptions and limitations: statutory permissions to copy

In this chapter you will learn about:

- copying which is not considered to be infringing
- important changes to the exceptions
- fair dealing
- the library regulations
- prescribed libraries
- declaration forms and electronic signatures
- charging for copying
- education exceptions
- judicial proceedings and other relevant exceptions
- copying for visually impaired persons.

What is meant by statutory permissions to copy

As well as protecting creators of original materials, copyright law also seeks to find a balance between the legitimate interests of creators of works and the needs of users to have access to such works. It is in the public interest for the law to be flexible enough to allow access and use of works in specific cases. Copyright is designed to encourage creativity so potential creators must be able to research the works of others, without fear of prosecution, in order to develop new ideas. Authors are not expected to buy every work in order to do research. Research and education are therefore valid reasons for copying. Governments, when drafting copyright laws, have to be extremely careful, however, to ensure that any exceptions and limitations to authors' rights do not prejudice the legitimate interests of authors to exploit their works. This is known as the copyright balance and is required under international conventions (see Chapter 8).

Certain specific acts of copying are not seen as infringing as long as the copying does not conflict with a normal exploitation of the work, and does not unreasonably prejudice the legitimate interests of authors. The Act, therefore, includes exceptions and limitations to the exclusive rights of authors. It is important to understand that users of copyright works do not have *rights* under copyright law, but *permissions* to copy. It is not seen as an infringement if one copies under a statutory exception but it must be borne in mind that this could always be challenged and may have to be defended in court if necessary, as rights holders may still object. Therefore, there is still a degree of risk attached to copying under a statutory exception.

There are many such exceptions in the UK Act, only some of which are covered in this section. The main exceptions (also called *permitted acts* or *statutory provisions*) relevant to the information profession are: a general permission to copy called fair dealing; copying for educational purposes; and copying by librarians and archivists. These are outlined in detail. Other relevant exceptions follow. Included in this section also are exceptions to performance rights.

The main exceptions relevant to information professionals

Important changes to note

The European Council Directive on the Harmonization of Copyright and Related Rights in the Information Society, familiarly called the Copyright Directive, has been implemented into UK law by the Copyright and Related Rights Regulations 2003. These regulations, which came into force on 31 October 2003, have detailed certain important changes to the Act which have had to be implemented in order to comply with the Copyright Directive and certain other Directives (see Chapter 8 for more details). These changes include the exceptions.

Arguably the most important change for information professionals is to the fair dealing exception which permits copying from a literary, dramatic, musical or artistic work for research or private study purposes. Under the original text of the Act, the purpose of research was not specified, so commercial research copying was permitted. It has since been decreed by the EU that exceptions should no longer allow any commercial (direct or indirect economic) gain, so changes have had to be made to outlaw any copying other than for a non-commercial purpose. Fair dealing is now limited to *research for a non-commercial purpose* or private study – and even copying for private study must not be for any direct or indirect commercial purpose.

The research limitation is also reflected in the library and archive regulations, so librarians from prescribed, not for profit, libraries or archives will no longer be able to supply a requested copy under these regulations to someone who requires the copy for research for a commercial purpose. Guidance on how this is to be interpreted is given in Chapter 4.

The acknowledgement requirement

Since the changes to the Act following the Copyright and Related Rights Regulations 2003, many of the exceptions include a condition that copies made should be sufficiently acknowledged unless this proves impracticable. This is defined (s. 178) as an identification of the work in question, whether published or unpublished, by its title or other description including its author unless the author chooses to remain anonymous, in the case of published works, or, for unpublished works, an attempt to identify the author by reasonable enquiry fails.

Making temporary copies (s. 28A)

This is a new exception to the Act. It was included in the Copyright Directive and was the only exception which all member states had to implement. It was necessary to include it as otherwise every time a work was transmitted over a network several infringing reproductions would have been made. This would have made little sense.

Temporary electronic copies of literary works (but not databases or computer programs), dramatic, musical or artistic works, the typographical arrangement of a published editions, sound recordings or films, e.g. copies held in a cache, do not infringe copyright. The conditions are that the copies held are transient or incidental to an integral and essential part of a technological process, and the sole purpose of this holding is to transmit the work in a network between third parties by an intermediary to enable a lawful use of the work or works. Such temporary copies should have no independent economic significance, otherwise they become infringing copies.

Fair dealing (ss. 29–30)

Fair dealing is a term, which, although is not defined as such, is generally accepted to mean a general permission to copy. As long as what is copied does not harm or prejudice the interests of rights holders then the person making the copies is usually copying under the defence of fair dealing. Fair dealing applies to specific purposes. *Dealing*, in this sense, is a form of general behaviour, and what is *fair* could only be decided in a court of law.

For private study

Copying from a literary work (including databases) or a dramatic, musical or artistic work for private study does not infringe any copyright in the work. Private study means exactly what it says: individual study for private purposes. Private study should be purely personal and should only benefit the person copying. The Act states that the definition of private study: 'does not include any study which is directly or indirectly for a commercial purpose' (s. 178). Such copying for these purposes is not restricted to hard-copy printed works, so a fair-dealing copy could be made from a literary, dramatic, musical or artistic work on the internet. Note this it is not applicable to sound recordings or films. Copies must be acknowledged as long as this is practicable.

For research for a non-commercial purpose

Copying from a literary, dramatic, musical or artistic work or from a database for research for a *non-commercial* purpose does not infringe any copyright in the work. Nor does it infringe copyright in the typographical arrangement of a published edition. The definition of research should not be confused with private study. Research is not defined but is generally seen to be a thorough investigation for the purpose of producing results for general or group use and is not undertaken for purely personal ends – its ends are usually intended for a group (however loosely defined). Fair dealing for these purposes is not restricted to hard-copy printed works, so a fair-dealing copy could be made from a literary, dramatic, musical or artistic work on the internet. Copies must be acknowledged as long as this is practicable.

A person may copy on another's behalf and any library may also copy on behalf of an individual under this provision (as well as under the library regulations; see below), but a librarian must not use fair dealing in order to copy more. Librarians are not allowed to make multiple copies under the library regulations so it follows that the same applies to fair dealing for private study or non-commercial research purposes.

For criticism or review

Anyone may copy from any type of work for the purposes of criticizing or reviewing a work or the work of another or of a performance of a work without infringing copyright. There are two conditions: the work must have been lawfully made available to the public, and the work must be sufficiently acknowledged. *Made available* for these purposes is defined as:

- the issuing of copies to the public
- making the work available by means of an electronic retrieval system
- the rental or lending of copies of the work to the public
- the performance, exhibition, playing or showing of the work in public
- the communication to the public of the work.

If criticizing or reviewing the work of an artist or photographer, a fair-dealing copy of an extract or even a whole work which has been made available to the public may be made for these purposes. These must be acknowledged, of course.

Students as well as reviewers may use this exception.

It is accepted that reviews are expected to be published, so copies made for criticism or review purposes may be published, including on the web. However, there may be difficulty in establishing whether publication on the web is fair, so it would be advisable not to copy a whole artistic work in order to criticize or review it unless it was in a very low resolution.

For news reporting

Anyone may make a copy from a work (but not photographs) for the purposes of reporting current events, provided sufficient acknowledgement is given (as long as this is practicable). This exception could be used for compilation of a current awareness bulletin using abstracts or annotations. It does not mean, however, that one is permitted under this provision to cut and copy newspaper articles and circulate them.

Copying by librarians and archivists (ss. 37–43 and SI 1989 No. 1212)

Library copying is governed by regulations known as the 'library regulations' or 'library privileges'. They apply to library staff of certain libraries who carry out photocopying on behalf of their users and for other libraries via an inter-library request.

Prescribed libraries

Only those libraries which are prescribed in the regulations, provided they are not part of an organization which is profit-making, are given these privileges. Those libraries which are listed in Figure 2.1, provided that they are not established or conducted for profit, are prescribed for the purposes of providing a copying service to the public under sections 38, 39 and 43, and for copying for archival or preservation purposes covered by sections 41 and 42, whether copying material from within their own stock, made for another non-profit based service, or received from another library. Some charitable or voluntary organizations may be confused as to whether they fall within this broad prescribed status. It is helpful to appreciate that as long as the library is *facilitating or encouraging the study of* any of the subjects listed under 'Other libraries', this fits the requirement. For example: a library of a charity dealing with human rights abuse is likely to be facilitating or encouraging the study of law or religion.

1   Public libraries
    Any library administered by:
    · public library authority in England and Wales
    · a statutory library authority in Scotland
    · an Education and Library Board in Northern Ireland.

2   National Libraries
    · British Library
    · National Library of Wales
    · National Library of Scotland
    · Bodleian Library, Oxford
    · University Library, Cambridge.

3   Libraries in educational establishments
    · a library of a school
    · libraries of universities which are empowered to award degrees
    · libraries of institutions providing further or higher education.

4   Parliamentary and government libraries

5   Local government libraries
    Any library administered by:
    · a local authority in England and Wales
    · a local authority in Scotland
    · a district council in Northern Ireland.

6   Other libraries
    · any library which encourages the study of bibliography, education, fine arts,
      history, languages, law, literature, medicine, music, philosophy, religion,
      science (including natural and social science) or technology
    · any library outside the UK which encourages the study of the above subjects.

Sources: SI 1989 No. 1068 and SI 1989 No. 1212.

Figure 2.1   Designated libraries prescribed to copy for certain purposes

Profit basis

The Act's phrase 'established or conducted for profit' applies to the parent organizations as well as to the services themselves, but the term is not defined. It
seems reasonable to assume that it means that the organization or service concerned has the objective of attaining an excess of income over expenditure. The

mere selling of services to recover a proportion of the expenditure, or even all the direct costs, without covering overheads and without making a true surplus, would not be construed as 'established or conducted for profit'. If a library service were split off as an independent business without subsidy, it would then become 'established or conducted for profit'. Obviously any library or information service operating in a commercial or industrial organization is unable to copy under these regulations as the organization is clearly run for profit.

Declaration forms

Librarians copying for their users are legally obliged under the Act to ask requesters to sign declaration forms before making the photocopies. The prescribed form is given in the regulations and is also reproduced in Appendix A. The declaration is to protect the librarian from accusations of infringement. The form may therefore be used as a defence and should be kept. Libraries must make their own judgement as to how long they should be kept, bearing in mind that accusations of infringement may be made for up to six years plus the alleged year of the making of the copy. However, to date there have been no court cases involving a librarian where a declaration has had to be produced.

Persons making requests have to declare that the material to be copied is either for the purposes of research for a non-commercial purpose, or for private study. A requester also has to declare on the form that a copy of the same material has not been supplied before, and that someone with whom they work or study has not requested (or is about to request) a copy of substantially the same material for substantially the same purpose. This means that if one person has been supplied with a photocopy of an item, the librarian may not make another copy of the same item for any of that person's colleagues. The reason behind all the bureaucracy is to prevent systematic single copying whereby several people make requests for the same items at about the same time. For example, if several students from the local college asked a public librarian for the same item for the same project, it should not be supplied under the library regulations. Systematic single copying is not seen to be fair by publishers.

The librarian must be satisfied that the information on the declaration forms is not false and that the request is valid. The form must be signed by the requester and be received by the librarian before the items are supplied. If the items were supplied before the form is received then there is a danger that the form would not be sent. The point about the declaration form protecting the librarian against accusation of infringement would then be negated.

As long as the conditions are met, declarations by fax are acceptable.

Electronic signatures

In the Electronic Communications Act 2000, which implemented the EU Electronic Signatures Directive, electronic signatures, or e-signatures, were made legally permissible in the UK.

In the library regulations it states that the signature of the person requiring a copy of a copyright item must be in 'writing'. 'Writing' is defined in the Act (s. 178) as including any form of notation or code, whether by hand or otherwise. It is believed, therefore, that the signature can be in electronic form. This argument is helped by the fact that the law does not require the exact wording of the declaration form A (see Appendix A) to be used, as long as the declaration is substantially the same as given in form A. However, the requirement is that the signature has to be personal. If the declaration form is received electronically how can a personal signature be achieved? The signature would have to clearly identify the individual and must not easily be used by others. Deciding what form of e-signature fulfils these criteria is a matter of opinion. The Electronic Signatures Directive defines 'electronic signature' to mean 'data in electronic form which are attached to or legally associated with other electronic data and which serve as a method of authentication'. This may be too broad a definition to satisfy the requirement for a personal signature. However, the Directive goes on to define an 'advanced electronic signature' which appears to satisfy a requirement for a personal signature as it has to be 'uniquely linked to and capable of identifying the signatory'.

Librarians may therefore receive declaration forms electronically as long as the personal signature requirement is fulfilled. This means that the signature has to have some unique link to the requester, e.g. via some form of authentication system. As there are no established standards to follow other than the extremely rigorous ones in existence for financial transactions, it is really up to each library to establish its own criteria for authentication appropriate for declaration forms and to test the water.

The charge for copying

Under the library regulations, librarians are required to charge the actual cost ('equivalent to but not exceeding') of making copies, including a 'contribution to the general expenses of the library attributable to its production'. No advice can be given as to the meaning of 'a contribution to the general expenses of the library' since it is undefined. A reasonable amount in the charges made to users, over and above the direct costs, to cover handling costs could be included. *This must not, however, be seen as a profit-making activity*. Photocopies obtained from other libraries may be paid for by the requesting library by using BLDSC request forms as currency. Libraries have to make their own decisions about how they effect the charging of the actual cost of making copies when obtained via interlibrary loan, as the Act offers no guidance on 'charging' users directly or recharging within the library budget margins. Some libraries offering current awareness services have introduced the device of accepting money in advance from requesting institutions and drawing from that deposit as requests are made. It is believed that this is an acceptable practice, although it cannot be regarded as authorized by the Act.

Note, however, that there is no statutory requirement to levy a charge when copying under the terms of a licence or for copies made under the fair-dealing provisions. Users making their own fair-dealing copies on self-operated photocopiers will, in many libraries, pay the cost involved either by inserting money in the machine or by paying for a photocopying 'credit card'. Such charges are neither required nor prevented by the Act.

Copying service (ss. 38–40)

Librarians and archivists may provide a copying service in response to local or interlibrary requests from individuals, subject to the prescribed conditions (declaration form plus charge – see above). Periodical articles and extracts from published literary, dramatic or musical (note, not artistic) works requested by library users for private study or non-commercial research purposes may be copied and supplied. Such copying is not seen as an infringement. Although artistic works are not included an illustration may be copied if it accompanies a work. Permission to copy under these provisions also includes copying the typographical arrangement.

Unlike fair dealing, where no indication of how much may be copied is given, the Act states that where copies are made and supplied to requesters, the amount of copying is limited to one article from an issue of a journal or periodical or a reasonable amount from a published edition. 'Reasonable amount' is whatever a requester thinks is reasonable and one could only be sure of what is reasonable if a case were tested in court of law. It is very unlikely that a rights holder will object if copying is limited to extracts of around 5% or a chapter from a work.

Copying for stock (s. 41)

Librarians from prescribed not-for-profit libraries are permitted to request single copies of items from another library to add to their collection, provided that certain conditions are met. Library staff may also supply copies to another library for the same purpose. The conditions are that where the request is for several articles from a periodical, or the whole or a substantial part of a book, the librarian has to state in writing that despite having made a reasonable attempt, they are unable to discover anyone to authorize the copying. An attempt must therefore be made beforehand to ask permission from whoever owns the copyright. If the librarian is unable to find the rights holder to ask permission, then such copying for stock may take place. Where the request is for a copy of just one article or for less than the whole or (substantial) part of a published work, there is no requirement to obtain written permission. The librarian making the copy is obliged to make a charge for the copy to recover the costs of production, plus a contribution towards the general expenses of the library (see above). Copies required for library stock may be obtained from the BLDSC or from any other library holding a copy. Copies obtained for stock, *even though they are photocopies*, are legitimate copies and may be placed in the library collection for use by researchers.

Copying for replacement or preservation (s. 42)

If it is not reasonably practical to buy another copy, librarians from prescribed not-for-profit libraries may make, or have made for them, a copy of a work from their reference collection in order to preserve it, if it is in danger of falling apart, or to replace it if it has been lost, destroyed or damaged. A library wishing to obtain a copy from another library must declare in writing that the copy requested is for reference only, that it is not reasonably practical to purchase it and that the work has been lost, destroyed or damaged. The library making the copy should make a charge for the copy plus a contribution towards the expenses of the service. 'Reasonably practical to purchase' has to be decided by the librarian. If it is available for purchase from the normal supplier then this must be considered as reasonable. However, if only a page or two needs replacing, it may not be reasonable to purchase a whole volume for just a few pages.

Copying unpublished works (s. 43)

Librarians of prescribed non-profit-based libraries are also allowed to copy the whole or part of certain unpublished literary, dramatic or musical works from documents held in the library or archive required for the purposes of research for a non-commercial purpose or private study, subject to the prescribed conditions. The requester must sign a declaration form. The declaration form (reproduced in Appendix B) is slightly different from the one for published works in that the requester must be reasonably sure that the document has not been published prior to being deposited in the library or archive, and that the copyright owner has not prohibited the copying of the work. Therefore, it is inferred that before allowing copying of unpublished works in a library or archive, permission should be obtained (where possible) from the author or author's estate before allowing any copying.

Exceptions for education

The following exceptions are applicable to educational establishments only. These are schools and other educational establishments which are defined by various education statutes – colleges of further and higher education and universities, etc. The exceptions do *not* apply to training departments within any other organization.

Copying for instruction (ss. 32 (1) and (2A))

The Act says that it is permitted to copy from a literary, dramatic, musical or artistic work in the course of instruction or preparation for instruction provided it is done by the person giving or receiving the instruction, it is not copied by means of a reprographic process, it is accompanied by a sufficient acknowledgement and copies made are for a non-commercial purpose. *A reprographic process* is defined as a process for making facsimile copies or involving the use of an appliance for making multiple copies. It includes any copying by electronic means but does not include the making of a film or sound recording. This indicates that copying from a literary or musical copyright work for such purposes is only allowed if it is done in longhand and not on a photocopier.

There is now a new section (s. 32 (2A)) which states that it is also permitted to copy for the purposes of instruction or preparation for instruction from a literary, dramatic or musical work which has been *made available* to the public. The definition of made available is the same as that for copying for criticism or review in section 30, i.e.:

- the issuing of copies to the public
- making the work available by means of an electronic retrieval system
- the rental or lending of copies of the work to the public
- the performance, exhibition, playing or showing of the work in public
- the communication to the public of the work.

The conditions are that such copying is fair dealing, is done by the person giving or receiving the instruction, is sufficiently acknowledged and is not done by means of a reprographic process. It is presumed this provision has been included to make it clear that internet copying is allowed for these purposes. An example could be downloading an item from the web to show to a class. However, no reprographic copying is allowed, so this would not extend to making copies of that item to give out as handouts.

Copying audiovisual material for teaching film and sound-recording production (s. 32 (2))

If an educational establishment runs courses on the making of films or film sound-tracks, then sound recordings, films and broadcasts may be copied in the course of, or in preparation for, instruction in the making of films or film sound-tracks, provided the copying is done by the person giving or receiving instruction, is accompanied by sufficient acknowledgement and is not for a commercial purpose. Any subsequent recorded 'products' made while taking advantage of this exception must not of course be dealt with i.e. sold or let for hire, otherwise they become infringing.

Copying for examinations (s. 32 (3))

It is not an infringement to copy for the purposes of examination by way of setting the questions, communicating the questions to the candidates, or answering the questions provided the questions are accompanied by sufficient acknowledgement unless this proves impractical or otherwise. This provision does not extend, however, to the reprographic copying of a musical work for use by an examination candidate in performing the work, so purchased copies must be used in this case. *Purposes of examination* is not defined but it is unlikely that this exemption applies to work continuously assessed as part of the examination process.

Copies made under section 32 must not be subsequently 'dealt with'. This means sold, let for hire or communicated to the public (other than allowed for the purposes of examination), otherwise they become infringing copies. For example, commercial publication or distribution of collections of past examination papers or extracts from them containing parts of copyright material is illegal unless permission is obtained.

Making an anthology for educational use (s. 33)

It is permitted to include a short passage, suitably acknowledged, from a published literary or dramatic work in an anthology which is intended for educational purposes in educational establishments and is described as such in any advertising material issued by or on behalf of the publisher, as long as the intended outcome consists mainly of material in which no copyright subsists – for example, a collection of out-of-copyright poems. No more than two excerpts may be included by the same author and published by the same publisher in any period of five years.

Performing a literary, dramatic or musical work (s. 34)

Permission is also given to educational establishments to perform literary, dramatic or musical works, or to play or show sound recordings, films or broadcasts, in the activities of the establishment or for the purposes of instruction. Such performances are not deemed to be public performances as long as the audience is restricted to teachers and pupils. It also means that, provided it is for instructional purposes, commercially produced videos may be shown in educational establishments, and so phrases such as 'licensed for home use only' or 'may not be performed in clubs, prisons or schools' may be ignored as long as the audience consists of students and those giving instruction only.

Playing music, other than to an audience of teachers and students, counts as a 'public performance' and will need to be licensed. For example, music played in exercise classes for people not registered as students or employees of an institution would almost certainly constitute a public performance. Public performances would need to be licensed by the Performing Right Society (PRS) and Phonographic Performance Ltd (PPL). See Chapter 6 on licensing solutions.

NB: artistic works are not included here because their display or exhibition does not infringe copyright.

Off-air recording for educational purposes (s. 35)

Off-air recording from broadcasts may be made by or on behalf of an educational establishment for non-commercial educational purposes without infringing copyright in the broadcasts and in any works contained in them. Such recordings must be acknowledged. Such recordings may be 'communicated to the public by a person situated within the premises of an educational establishment provided that the communication cannot be received by any person situated outside the premises of that establishment'. Recordings may not be dealt with as otherwise they become infringing recordings. 'Dealt with' means sold or let for hire, offered or exposed for sale or hire, or communicated from within the premises of an educational establishment to any person situated outside those premises.

However, the above permission does not apply if there is a certified licensing scheme available. At present there are two licensing schemes (see Chapter 6, pages 113–15) covering terrestrial broadcasts, so copying these will be under the terms of the licences. Satellite and cable channels, however, provided they are legitimately received, may be recorded for educational purposes as there is no licensing scheme available.

Reprographic copying (s. 36)

An educational establishment may make reprographic copies from published literary, dramatic or musical works, including the typographic arrangement of published editions, for the purposes of instruction provided that the instruction is for a non-commercial purpose and the copies are sufficiently acknowledged unless this proves impractical. Only 1% of any work in any quarterly period, i.e. 1 January to 31 March, 1 April to 30 June, etc., may be copied. If, however, there is a licensing scheme which covers such copying then this exception is no longer applicable as an educational establishment is expected to take out such a licence and comply with its terms. There are licensing schemes available covering published literary and dramatic works (see Chapter 6 for details). Although all educational establishments are licensed by the CLA, the exception could apply to those works excluded from the CLA licence repertoire. Also, there is at present no licensing scheme which covers musical works so this exception could apply to these works.

Computer programs: permitted acts (ss. 29 (4), 50A, 50B, 50BA and 50C)

Computer programs are classed as literary works and so the fair-dealing exceptions, in theory, apply. The Act makes a point of stating what is not fair dealing with a computer program, and then later on points out that such acts are permitted – with conditions of course. This can be confusing.

For example, section 29 (4) states that it is not fair dealing to convert a computer program expressed in a low level language into a version expressed in a higher level. It is not fair dealing to copy a program in the process of converting it. Also, in section 29 (4)(a) it states that it is not fair dealing to observe, study or test the functioning of a computer program in order to determine the ideas and principles which underlie any element of the program. However, all these are acts which are permitted in sections 50A, 50B and 50BA. In brief, these sections clarify that a lawful user of a copy of a computer program is allowed:

- to make a back-up copy of a computer program if this is necessary even if terms or conditions state otherwise
- to copy or adapt a program, provided that the copying or adapting is necessary for lawful use and is not prohibited under contract
- to observe, study or test a program by any device or means
- to decompile the program to the extent necessary to achieve interoperability of an independently created program with other programs.

The definition of a lawful user of a computer program is a person who has a right to use the program, whether by licence or otherwise.

Databases: permitted acts (s. 50D)

Databases are subject to copyright and database right (see Chapter 1, page 5).

The Act states in section 50D that lawful users of a database are authorized to do anything necessary to enable them to access and use the contents. The regulations state that 'it is not an infringement of *copyright* in a database for a person who has a right to use the database or any part of the database (whether under licence to do any of the acts restricted by the copyright in the database or otherwise)', i.e. a lawful user, 'to do, in the exercise of that right, anything which is necessary for the purposes of access to and use of the contents of the database or of that part of the database'. It is also stated that, even if there is a term or condition in any contract which accompanies the database which purports to prohibit or restrict this lawful use, this can be ignored.

Database right exceptions (SI 1997 No. 3032)

The following concerns the exceptions from *database right* only.

It is an infringement of database right if someone extracts and reutilizes a *substantial* part of the contents without authorization. However, lawful users are allowed to extract or reutilize *insubstantial* parts of a database which has been made available to the public in any manner. NB: repeated or systematic extraction or reutilization of insubstantial parts could amount to a substantial part and thus an infringement. Also, the regulations state that, for avoidance of doubt, any term or condition in any agreement (licence) to use such a database which prevents such extraction or reutilization shall be void.

An exception is given to extracting a *substantial part* of the contents if the extraction is undertaken by a lawful user and it is extracted for the purpose of illustration for teaching or research and not for any commercial purpose. The source must also be indicated. NB: this exception covers only extraction and not reutilization. Reutilization means 'making the contents of a database available to the public by any means'.

There are also exceptions for copying for Parliamentary and judicial proceedings; Royal Commission and statutory enquiries; material open to public inspection or on an official register; material communicated to the Crown in the course of public business; public records; and acts done under statutory authority. These are similar to those under copyright. However, there is no specific library copying permission which applies to database right covering extraction/reutilization for research or private study. In any case, the changes following the implementation of the Copyright Directive imply that such copying may take place for non-commercial research purposes or private study.

Parliamentary and judicial proceedings exception (s. 45)

Copyright is not infringed by copying for the purposes of Parliamentary or judicial proceedings. The term 'judicial proceedings' is defined as including 'proceedings before any court, tribunal or person having authority to decide any matter affecting a person's legal rights or liabilities', and 'Parliamentary proceedings' is defined as including proceedings of the Northern Ireland Assembly, the Scottish Parliament or the European Parliament, as well as the UK Parliament.

In the case of judicial proceedings, although there is nothing in the Act, it is generally accepted to refer to copying only after the issuing of a writ. Copyright is not infringed by anything done for the purposes of reporting such proceedings, but this does not extend to authorizing the copying of a work which is itself a published report of the proceedings.

The law assumes that copying is undertaken by the person who wants the copy or copies. However, sometimes librarians will be asked to copy material for this purpose and the librarian may insist on the requester signing a declaration form and making a charge, even though there is absolutely no legal requirement to do so. This is entirely a matter of library policy and is understandable because of potential liability problems, but a librarian should not bind a requester by including restrictions on the form which are not required. For example, it is not necessary to make requesters sign to say that they have not had the copy before and that someone with whom they work or study has not asked for the same material at about the same time for the same purpose. In other words, the declaration form used for copying for research or private study is not appropriate in this case.

Copying by and for visually impaired persons (ss. 31A–E)

The original UK Act did not have any specific exceptions to allow copying for, or by, blind or partially sighted persons. Of course, visually impaired persons may take advantage of existing exceptions such as fair dealing, but this restricts the amount to be copied by or for a visually impaired person (VIP). A VIP may need a whole work copied into Braille or read onto tape, and this is not covered by fair dealing. Such copying has had to be authorized with permission from rights holders, which is time-consuming. The Publishers Licensing Society, the Authors' Licensing and Collecting Society and other publishing and licensing organizations collaborated with the RNIB on some very useful guidelines on copying by and for visually impaired persons (see Chapter 10, pages 171). However, there were still considerable drawbacks. VIPs felt they were being disadvantaged and preferred to copy lawfully with statutory permission rather than by voluntary agreement.

The EU Copyright Directive allowed an exception for people with disabilities. However, although the UK Government was willing to consider such an exception, it was unable to do so in the implementation process. Encouraged by the RNIB and other supporting organizations, including CILIP, a private member's bill was introduced into Parliament in 2002. The Copyright (Visually Impaired Persons) Act 2002 received royal assent and became law on 31 October 2003. The 1988 Act has been amended to reflect the changes.

The Copyright (Visually Impaired Persons) Act introduced two exceptions to copyright that provide solutions to access problems for visually impaired persons, one for individual VIPs and the other for making multiple copies. Copies made for VIPs are called *accessible* copies and they can be in any format according to the access needs of VIPs, e.g. Braille, Moon, digital, enlarged print, or recorded onto tape or CD.

Individual VIPs

A visually impaired person (a definition has to be established) may make a single accessible copy of a copyright work for personal use, subject to a number of conditions. One of these conditions is that the VIP must be in lawful possession of, or be able to lawfully use, the item in question. For example, if a VIP has purchased, or has borrowed from a library, a work which he or she is unable to read because the print is far too small, the VIP is allowed to copy, or have someone else copy, the work into large print in order to be able to access it. If, however, there is a commercially available large print version of that particular work which is suitable for that VIP, then the exception does not apply as the work can be purchased or borrowed in that format. However, even though an accessible version is available commercially, it may not suit every VIP, e.g. the print may still be too small or the audio version may not have navigation aids. If this is the case, then the fact that a commercial copy is available can be ignored.

The accessible copy is for personal use and may only remain in the VIP's possession as long as the VIP lawfully holds the original version (master copy), so if the book has been borrowed from a library, the book and the accessible copy have to be returned by the due date. If other VIPs wish to read the accessible copy, they may only do so if they are in lawful possession of the original version, so a VIP may loan his or her accessible copy to another VIP friend or colleague as long as that friend or colleague has a master copy as well.

The other conditions are:

- only changes necessary for the particular visual impairment may be made
- the exception does not apply to copying databases or performances of musical works
- accessible copies must be acknowledged, where possible, and bear the legend

'copied under s. 31A of the Copyright, Designs and Patents Act 1988'
- no-one must profit from the activity.

The multiple-copy exception

Educational establishments as defined under section 174 of the Act, or bodies not conducted for profit, may make multiple accessible copies of a literary, dramatic, musical or artistic work or a published edition and supply them to VIPs for their personal use, on condition that:

- the educational establishment or body is not conducted for profit and is in possession of a master copy
- copies are made for educational purposes
- accessible copies are not supplied to anyone who has access to a suitable commercially available copy in the desired format
- only changes necessary for the particular visual impairment are made
- databases or performances of musical works are not copied
- accessible copies are acknowledged and bear the legend 'copied under s. 31B of the Copyright, Designs and Patents Act 1988'
- rights holders are notified that such copies have been made within a reasonable time from making the accessible copies under the exception
- if there is a licensing scheme which covers this activity, licences under that scheme are taken out (the CLA now has a licensing scheme – see Chapter 6, page 102).

Accessible copies must not be dealt with, i.e. sold or let for hire, or offered to be sold or hired or communicated to the public on a network. The same sanctions for copyright infringement apply. See Chapter 7, pages 121–2.

Other relevant exceptions

Copying abstracts (s. 60)

The Act says that abstracts which accompany scientific or technical articles in periodicals may be copied freely and issued to the public, e.g. in current awareness leaflets. However, this would not cover abstracts copied from abstracting bulletins. An abstracting bulletin would be classed as a database.

Incidental inclusion (s. 31)

If a copyright work is included incidentally in an artistic work, sound recording, film or broadcast, copyright is not infringed. An example of this might be the making of a video in which a work of art was on display. Also such resulting works, provided they have been lawfully created, may be issued to the public, played, shown or communicated to the public.

Royal Commission or statutory inquiry (s. 46)

Copyright is not infringed by anything done for the purposes of the proceedings of a Royal Commission or statutory inquiry.

Public inspection (s. 47)

Material open to public inspection for statutory purposes (e.g. planning documents lodged with a local authority) may be copied, subject to certain conditions.

Anonymous or pseudonymous works (s. 57)

Copying is allowed from a literary, dramatic, musical or artistic work if, after reasonable enquiry, it proves impossible to ascertain the identity of the author (or authors if there is joint authorship), and where it is reasonable to assume the copyright has expired or that the author or authors died over 70 years ago. This does not apply to works protected by the Crown or certain international organizations.

Reading in public (s. 59)

The reading or recitation in public by one person of a reasonable extract from a published literary or dramatic work does not infringe copyright as long as it is acknowledged. Also such a reading or recitation may be recorded or communicated to the public as long as the recording or communication to the public consists of lawful material.

It would be wise to obtain permission from the publishers in the case of formally organized events as opposed to informal readings. It is unlikely that reading a whole children's picture book in a public library would be seen as an infringement.

Advertising art works for sale (s. 63)

Copies may be made and issued to the public of artistic works in order to advertise them for sale. This would include the compilation of such works in a catalogue. Copies made under this exception must not later be sold or let for hire or communicated to the public, otherwise they become infringing copies.

Playing of sound recordings in clubs (s. 67)

Clubs, societies or other organizations, as long as they are not established or conducted for profit and their main objectives are charitable or concerned with the advancement of religion, education or social welfare, are allowed to play sound recordings as part of their activities without infringing copyright. The sound recordings may not be played by anyone with a view to gain e.g. disc jockeys. Also, no profit must be made from any events where such sound recordings are played: any proceeds from charges for admission have to be ploughed back into the organization solely for the benefit of the organization, and any proceeds made from any goods or services sold at events where sound recordings are played have to be similarly used.

Off-air recording for time-shifting purposes (s. 70)

The private and domestic copying of a broadcast (e.g. making a video of a TV programme, or a tape of a radio programme, for use at a more convenient time) is allowed. This is familiarly called time-shifting. Recordings must be made on domestic premises and they must not be subsequently dealt with, i.e. they must not be sold or let for hire, offered or exposed for hire or communicated to the public, otherwise they become infringing copies.

Photograph of a broadcast (s. 71)

A photograph or slide of the whole or part of an image forming part of a broadcast, or a copy of the photograph, may be made on domestic premises for private and domestic use only. This does not apply to videos or DVDs. Such photographs may not subsequently be dealt with, i.e. they must not be sold or let for hire, offered or exposed for hire or communicated to the public, otherwise they become infringing copies.

Free public showing or playing of a broadcast (s. 72)

As long as the public is not charged for admission to wherever the showing is to take place, this is allowed. This mainly applies to clubs or societies which are not run for profit, or residents and inmates of an institution. So, for example, an NHS hospital may put the television or radio on for the patients. The use of music sound recordings in the broadcasts is outside this exception, however, and needs to be licensed. Notification of such a licensing scheme has to be made to the Secretary of State (s. 128A).

Sculptures, buildings and works of artistic craftsmanship on public display (s. 62)

A representation may be made of works which are on permanent public display, e.g. a statue in the park or a building, or situated in premises open to the public. Representation means taking a photograph or film of the work, making a graphic work, or making a broadcast of a visual image of it. Nor is it an infringement to issue to the public or to communicate to the public copies of such works. The resulting work, e.g. a photograph or a work of art, attracts a new copyright for the photographer or artist.

Ten things to remember from this chapter

- users do not have any rights to copy; rights belong to authors
- copying under a statutory exception could still be challenged
- copying under fair dealing for commercial research is no longer permitted
- systematic single copying or multiple copying is not considered fair
- only not-for-profit libraries may copy under the library regulations
- library-copying declaration forms must be received before supplying items
- librarians are not allowed to copy artistic works under the library regulations
- no declaration forms are needed when copying for judicial proceedings
- videos may be shown in schools, etc., as long as the audience is not public
- there are now exceptions for visually impaired persons to make copies and have copies made for them.

3 Public lending

In this chapter you will learn about:

- the law relating to rental and lending
- the difference between rental and lending
- obligations on public libraries
- LA/BPI Agreement to allow the lending of music sound recordings
- lending other material in public libraries.

Rental and lending legislation

The Act of 1988 established a new and separate right for rental services (s. 18), including public lending. Public lending was separated from rental right with the Copyright and Related Rights Regulations 1996 (SI 1996 No. 2967) which implemented the European Council Directive on Rental and Lending No. 92/100/EEC. An exclusive right was given to authors, artists, dramatists, composers, performers and producers of sound and video recordings. and producers and principal directors of films, to authorize or prohibit rental and lending of their productions. This affected the lending of all books, artistic materials including maps, printed music, sound and video recordings, CD-ROMs and computer software.

Definition of rental

The term *rental* means 'making a copy of a work available for use, on terms that it will or may be returned for direct or indirect commercial advantage'. In other words, rental is hiring works out for profit.

Definition of lending

Lending is defined to mean the making of a copy of the work available for use, on terms that it will or may be returned, otherwise than for direct or indirect economic or commercial advantage, through an establishment which is accessible to the public. It excludes lending: between establishments which are accessible to the public; for on-the-spot reference use; or for the purpose of public performance, playing or showing in public, and communicating to the public. 'Direct or indirect economic or commercial advantage' does not necessarily mean that lending becomes rental if a charge is made for the service. As long as the charge does not go beyond what is necessary to cover the operating costs of the establishment, a charge may be made for lending. It is important to note that the vast majority, if not all, public libraries are engaged in the activity of *lending* and not rental.

None of the new rights apply to existing copies acquired before 1 December 1996 for the purpose of lending to the public, and no lending done before 1 December 1996 is to be regarded as an infringement of any lending right.

The need for authorization for lending and renting

The regulations apply to public libraries as defined in the Public Libraries and Museums Act 1964, the Public Libraries (Scotland) Act 1955 or the Education and Libraries (Northern Ireland) Order 1986. So public libraries need to be authorized to lend, and must obtain the necessary authorization from those who hold the lending rights. To date this has not been at all straightforward, and negotiations to make public libraries legal continue.

Lending rights may still be with the authors but it is more likely that they have been assigned to their publishers/producers along with all the other necessary rights needed to publish. In any case, it is normally their publishers and producers that libraries have to deal with when negotiating a licence to lend. The EU Directive permitted derogation to be made in respect of the grant of exclusive lending rights as long as at least authors and performers are remunerated in respect of lending. Authors and performers can, therefore, insist that some licensing fee be paid by libraries for the act of lending their material. However, it is understood that they may only claim such remuneration from their publishers/producers, as part of their contract, and not directly from the library, so the onus is on their publishers/producers to negotiate for them.

If the owners of lending rights refuse to license such rights to libraries, the Secretary of State for Trade and Industry has the power to order rights holders to license the lending of literary, dramatic, musical or artistic works, sound recordings or films subject to payment of a reasonable royalty (s. 66). Also, the Copyright Tribunal (see Chapter 7, page 126) may be invoked to determine what is a reasonable royalty where compulsory licensing has been ordered.

Exceptions to lending right

Libraries in educational establishments and other non-profit prescribed libraries or archives are permitted to lend works and so do not need authorization (ss. 36A and 40A (2)). However, should there be restrictions on lending attached to purchasing agreements, it should be made clear to the supplier that the material is to be lent and that the organization is not prohibited by law to lend. If the supplier refuses to supply on those terms then the library has the option of deciding to buy something else or negotiating. However, any library that rents copyright works (i.e. making a profit) definitely needs authorization to do so.

Public library lending

The lending of books and other printed matter

Section 40A states that copyright is not infringed by the lending of a book by a public library if the book is within the public lending right scheme. So, the lending of books by public libraries needs no further authorization as it is covered by the remunerations to authors under the Public Lending Right (PLR) scheme, provided that such books are eligible and are covered by the definition of 'book' as defined by the scheme: any book with printed text which could also contain illustrations. Another definition is that to be eligible, the work must have an ISBN.

Any other printed matter lent by public libraries which is not covered by the PLR scheme should, ideally, be covered by a licence to lend.

Lending music sound recordings

There has been a licence available for lending sound recordings of music from BPI member companies since 1994. An approach was made by The Library Association to the British Phonographic Industry (BPI) in 1989 for authorization to lend music sound recordings. The BPI represents some 330 companies providing about 80–90% of recorded music output in the UK. A list of BPI members is on its website. The UK is the second biggest recorded music producer in the world. The BPI was very nervous at first about disturbing its market and so was reluctant to agree to any scheme, but after lengthy discussion spanning several years, the industry was finally persuaded to allow the lending of music sound recordings. The negotiations between the BPI and the LA resulted in the LA being licensed to grant sub-licences to public library authorities, royalty-free but subject to certain conditions. The BPI was not particularly interested in administering a licensing scheme and collecting payments so was happy for the LA to take over the administration and make the licence royalty-free. Libraries regularly lending such recordings should be licensed under this scheme. Contact CILIP for details.

The LA/BPI Agreement

The main terms of the licence (soon to be the CILIP/BPI Agreement) are set out below.

1 Signatory libraries are licensed to lend sound recordings in vinyl, cassette or compact disc format. This really needs updating as most libraries lend digital material and the lending of vinyl is rare.
2 A maximum of four copies per recording is allowed per service point currently providing recordings for loan. No more than two of those copies are to be in any one format. For example, if only CDs are purchased then a public library may only buy and lend two copies per service point. If cassettes are purchased as well, then the public library may purchase two copies in the CD format and two in cassette format per service point.
3 A 'holdback' on new releases is imposed for three months for all formats. This means that the library may purchase a newly released recording but the recording may not be lent until three months after the date of release. When deciding what may or may not be covered by the holdback, it is useful to remember that the over-riding reason for the holdback is so that the industry can maximize on sales during that time. Although classical labels are covered, it is more critical to the popular labels, i.e. chart material. The BPI has said that the holdback does not apply to the same title re-released on a different format, but it has confirmed that it does apply to re-released titles by the same company either on the same or on a different label, so compilations of various artists will be covered, as will greatest hits collections. It also applies to American import albums if they have been exclusively licensed to a BPI member. Therefore, the majority of chart material will be covered by this. Each BPI member is free to decide for which titles, if any, the holdback would be waived.
4 The limitation on the number of copies per service point is subject to the 'swings and roundabouts' accumulation provision whereby smaller service points acquiring fewer copies compensate for larger service points acquiring more, provided that the total for the authority as a whole does not exceed the number per service point. For example, if the public library has ten service points and buys only CDs, the limit on the number of copies purchased is 10 x 2 = 20 but these could be distributed among only eight of them or even just one depending on where the demand is.
5 The same 'swings and roundabouts' provision applies to the limitation per format.
6 The agreement is renewed automatically every year.
7 The BPI and the LA agreed to co-operate on publicity about the provision of the copyright legislation in respect of home taping and the restrictions

outlined above. CILIP has produced a poster for licensed users to place by a recordings collection. Contact CILIP for details.

8   The BPI and the LA agreed to co-operate on a study of the nature and use of recordings collections in public libraries. To date, despite promptings, there has been no research undertaken.

9   Recordings are lent on the understanding that they are for private, domestic or educational use only. Recordings may be lent to schools or other educational establishments for teachers to play to students as long as the performance is not public. However, they must never be lent to commercial establishments for playing in public, e.g. in a public house, in a retail establishment or on a radio station.

Further negotiations

The agreement has been in place for many years now and the BPI has accepted and publicly stated that public library music services are for the general public benefit, and that it benefits both sides for libraries to continue to lend discs and disseminate recorded music. Several changes are necessary to update the present agreement. To begin with, the LA is no longer a legal entity and so the agreement needs to incorporate CILIP. The agreement needs to extend to other digital formats now being lent, such as music DVDs. Also, it is necessary to look at the agreement in the light of other future library services, such as the provision of listener points and accessibility to music in libraries over the internet. CILIP has approached the BPI to consider these issues.

Non-BPI members

There is no scheme which authorizes the lending of sound recordings from non-BPI members at present. It is understood that the rights holders are not interested in licensing public libraries, probably because of the administration involved, and so until such times as they do, the material may be lent freely and without restrictions. As always, public libraries should make it clear, when purchasing, that the material is to be lent and if supplied under those terms, an implied licence is granted.

Lending spoken-word material

Most spoken-word recordings are not covered by the LA/BPI Agreement either, so, again for public libraries to lend this material legally, there has to be some other permission or licence. Negotiations have taken place over the years between the LA and various representatives of authors, performers and publishers of spoken-word material to try to resolve the lending situation. Some spoken-word publishers have said that they supply recordings with a licence to lend as they have been assigned lending rights in their contracts with the authors and performers. Other spoken-word publishers say that they do not hold lending rights, and libraries are lending illegally unless they pay for a licence. Author and performer representatives have said that they want remuneration for lending. At present there are no negotiated licences. In the meantime, until the situation is resolved, public libraries lending spoken-word material are advised that when purchasing recordings it should be made clear in purchase orders that the material is to be lent. If orders are supplied on those terms then lending can take place.

CILIP believes that, as the Government votes PLR payments to authors for the lending of their printed output, the Government should legislate to extend PLR to cover their spoken output, and many agree that this is a sensible solution. Attempts have been made to persuade the Government to include spoken-word material in the PLR remit. To date this has not been successful. The 2002 review of PLR concluded that this should be looked at in future, and the Government has set up an advisory committee to examine the possibility. Lending spoken-word material has always been difficult because performers' rights have to be considered, as well as those of authors. The Government does not remunerate performers under PLR.

Lending films (videocassettes and DVDs)

There is no licence available from video producers for lending videos and DVDs. The video recording industry's attitude to licensing appears to differ from that of the sound recording industry. In the past, the LA has offered several times to negotiate with the industry body, the British Video Association, but there seems to be no wish to disturb the commercial rental market by interposing a licensing system other than the present method of charging appropriately at the point of sale, e.g. on rental versions of the product.

CILIP recommends that public libraries should adhere to the terms of any contracts with video producers and report to CILIP if problems arise. A charge may be made for the lending but there should be no intention of making a profit. The Act says that there should be 'no direct or indirect economic or commercial advantage'.

Where there are two versions of the product for sale simultaneously, i.e. retail and rental, preferably the rental should always be purchased. Sometimes the rights holder will stipulate that retail versions may not be lent. CILIP sometimes receives complaints from video rental outlets about the competition from their local library – the library is obviously undercutting the rental outlet. If the products are bought under the same terms, i.e. rental versions, the library is not working under an unfair advantage. If not, these complaints may be justified. Where the retail version is not released until after the rental version has been out for some time, the library must use its discretion about which version to purchase, bearing in mind the above.

As with sound recordings, videos should be lent on the understanding that they are for private, domestic or educational use only. They should never be used for a public performance. Some video producers have shown concern in the past that lending to residential homes for the elderly constitutes a public performance. Therefore, it is advised that, if there is reason to believe that the performance will be in a public area, the video is loaned for use by individual residents rather than to the institution itself.

Lending computer software

Any public libraries wishing to lend software packages should be authorized. There is no blanket licensing scheme so any negotiation has to be directly with producers. This may not be forthcoming as many software producers contractually forbid rental or lending in their dubious 'shrink-wrapped' bound contracts.

Lending mixed media (books with discs)

Many publications, such as open learning material, have accompanying software or CD-ROMs. It should be made clear in the purchase order if the package is being purchased for lending purposes. If it is supplied without further comment, then there has been some implied consent to the lending. If books are ordered and delivered with unsolicited accompanying discs plus user licence, clarification on lending and use should be sought from the publisher. If the producer/publisher says the disc cannot be lent, then there are three options: the package can be used solely within the premises; the disc or other media can be removed and the book or other print material lent on its own; or the package can be returned as not fit for purpose under the Supply of Goods (Implied Terms) Act. For those packages already purchased, the conditions of supply should be checked, if necessary by writing to each producer/publisher. It should be made clear on the package that the disc or other media may not be copied (unless of course the software/media is in the public domain or permission has been given with the package).

Lending CD-ROMs

CD-ROMs and other forms of optical digital media are also subject to the rental and lending restriction. Not all CD-ROM products are suitable for lending. For those that are, it is advised that permission to offer a lending service is obtained from each publisher. Order forms should make it clear that the product is being purchased for the library as part of the lending stock. On items already purchased, the contract of sale should be examined to see whether there is any restriction on lending. If there is, then the options are either to return the product under the terms of the Supply of Goods (Implied Terms) Act as not fit for purpose, or to cease lending. The multimedia company Ramesis, which is administered by Chivers (see Appendix C, page 178, for details) supplies public libraries with CD-ROMs which are all cleared for lending.

Lending music scores and maps

Other material such as printed music and maps should in theory be licensed for lending. There are no such umbrella licensing schemes available, so discretion should be used. However, as lending is not defined to include the making available of a work for public performance, the lending of music scores for that purpose may not need to be covered. Ordnance Survey allow the lending of their maps under the OS Service Level Agreement.

Ten things to remember from this chapter

- rental and lending are restricted acts
- public libraries lend not rent
- public libraries must be authorized to lend
- there is no restriction on lending between public libraries
- prescribed not-for-profit libraries and educational establishments are exempt from certain lending restrictions
- the lending of books in public libraries is covered by PLR
- the licensing of spoken-word recordings is still unresolved
- where authorization is in doubt, libraries should make it clear in purchasing contracts that items are to be lent
- a library always has the option of returning a purchase if lending is forbidden
- discretion must be used when deciding on the purchase of a rental or a retail video or DVD.

4 Copyright compliance: statutory solutions

In this chapter you will learn about:

- whether copying is authorized under a statutory exception
- the test of fairness
- the test for what is commercial and what is non-commercial research
- limits of copying and use under a statutory exception
- staying legal when copying from various materials.

To help information professionals and their users to keep on the right side of the law, this chapter and the following two chapters are on copyright compliance. This chapter elaborates on the statutory permissions outlined in Chapter 2 and includes guidance on the limits of copying and use under an exception, and whether such copying needs to pass a test of fairness. As has been seen, statutory copying is not without risk. Such copying could still be challenged. If, after reading Chapter 2 and this chapter, it is concluded that there are far too many risks in following statutory conditions of copying or even that they do not apply to your situation, then a decision has to be made either to stop any copying malpractice, or to seek another compliance solution such as obtaining permission or a licence.

The need for authorization before copying

Authorization is needed for *any* copying of copyright-protected material or material protected by database right. When in doubt, the question must be asked whether the copying is authorized by statute, permission, contract or licence. This chapter deals with the authorization given by statute. The following two chapters will concentrate on licensing and contracts.

Now that the restrictions on copying for indirect or direct commercial purposes has been implemented into the Act, not only must a user decide whether the purpose of copying is authorized (e.g. am I allowed to copy under fair dealing still?), a user must consider whether the copying is fair or reasonable. There are likely to be limits on the amounts copied and one must ask whether these are going to harm the interests of rights holders. Hopefully, this chapter will provide enough information to guide users, and information professionals who copy for their users, to keep within the confines of the law.

When copying starts to become unfair, then other compliance solutions have to be considered. However, as perceptions of what is fair or unfair may differ, it is useful to lay down some parameters. The copying and use limits given in this chapter have long been recognized by the profession as being fair and should not harm the interests of authors and rights holders. In any disputed copying, a court of law would have to decide. Most organizations would want to avoid this scenario.

Tests of fairness

It may be helpful to follow an information professional's two-step test (as opposed to the Berne Convention's three-step test – see Chapter 8, pages 139–40) of fairness on whether one is entitled to make a copy. This applies mainly to copying for non-commercial research or private study. Copying under other exceptions is not so much of a problem. For example, copying for the purposes of Parliamentary or judicial proceedings or any other of the public administration exceptions is not limited to amounts or qualified by the commercial restriction, nor is the copying of abstracts or copying for the purposes of examination in education. Other exceptions are carefully defined, so one can establish easily whether they apply. This is not so with the general fair-dealing permission which is so vague.

Step 1: authorization

The first question to be asked is what is the purpose of copying? Is it authorized under an exception in the Act?

There are several permitted purposes in the Act, as has been seen in Chapter 2, e.g. copying:

(a) for private study
(b) for research for a non-commercial purpose
(c) to criticize another's work
(d) to review another's work
(e) for instruction
(f) for examination
(g) for Parliamentary or judicial proceedings
(h) for those with a visual impairment.

Step 2: purpose

If one is copying under (a) or (b), one may not copy a substantial amount as this would infringe. It is important to bear in mind that *substantial* can mean in a qualitative as well as quantitative sense, so what is intended to be copied could well be judged substantial in a court of law even though the amount copied may be very small. So, although there may be no way of knowing whether even a small amount will infringe at the time of copying, one can ask questions about whether the act of copying is likely to harm the rights holder, for example:

- Am I copying in order to profit directly or indirectly by it?
- Am I copying instead of buying it?
- Would I have bought it if I could not copy it?
- Am I planning to make several copies of the same item?
- Are my colleagues likely to be copying the same item for the same purpose?
- Is the integrity of the work being damaged by my copying it?

If the answer to all of these questions is 'no', then there should be no problem. If the answer to any of them is 'yes', then another solution should be sought, such as obtaining authorization from the rights holders. See the following two chapters.

If copying for research, a user may question the distinction between research for a commercial and a non-commercial purpose. This may cause problems for the information professional and concern has already been expressed within the profession about telling the difference. However, *it is essential to bear in mind that the responsibility for copying lies with the person wishing to make a copy*, and only that person can and should judge the purpose; and when the copy is made under the library regulations, librarians can still rely on the signed declaration forms. It would be extremely unwise, therefore, for librarians and information staff to quiz requesters on the purpose of copying or give unsolicited advice, as the librarian could be held responsible if the declaration later turns out to be false. It is also not a good idea to stand over the copier or in any way supervise the copying. That said, however, librarians as part of the information profession must act professionally and be seen to be acting professionally. The Government and rights holders expect it. A careful path must be taken, therefore, between turning a blind eye and giving advice.

It would be unprofessional not to help a user if guidance were requested. Copyright policy should help determine the extents of such guidance. A user, may simply require advice on the changes to the law. In any case it is sensible, and will be expected in public places, for posters to be mounted at or near copying machines pointing out general guidance on copying which incorporates the changes. See Chapter 7, pages 123–6 for liability issues.

However, if users *ask* for guidance on whether their copying is legitimate, the above fairness questions can be asked and Figure 4.1 can be shown to them, but it should be made absolutely clear that the responsibility for copying lies with them. It is NOT advisable to decide for a user whether their copying is legitimate. Advice given, even in good faith, that later proves to be wrong could result in legal liability.

Whether the copying is commercial or not will largely depend on the *purpose at the time of copying*. Why is the copy required at this present time? Any future and (unforeseen) purpose can be ignored. It should not be assumed that just because copying takes place in a for-profit company that all copying for research will be commercial, although it is likely that the majority of it will be. For example, someone in a commercial company may well wish to make a copy of an item which might later be useful in dealing with a client. At the time, the copying may have been for research for a non-commercial purpose and so legitimate. Later uses were not foreseen. Conversely, it is likely that some research in a higher education institution may well be for indirect commercial research purposes, and that purpose is known at the time of copying. Any copying would therefore have to be authorized by licence or with permission as it would not come under fair dealing.

To help users make a decision, here are some examples of private study, non-commercial research and commercial research. *NB: These are examples for guidance only and not set in stone*. The ultimate test, of course, would be if a case came to court.

Private study
- Work done by any person for their own personal or professional development (as long as there is no direct or indirect commercial purpose).
- Work done by students for their courses, whether full time or on day release from their employer (but this work must not benefit the employer financially).

Non-commercial research
- Research undertaken by lecturers for teaching purposes. This may exclude the creation of commercial by-products, such as e-learning materials.
- Research in drafting an article for a scholarly journal for which no payment is expected.
- Work done by lecturers or students as part of a research project even if it is sponsored by a commercial company, as long as the prime aim of the organization undertaking the research is educational.
- Work done in preparation for a conference speech where no payment is expected.
- Work done to assist in NHS services.
- Work done by a student on a taught course. If the student happens to receive sponsorship by a company and has to work for them after graduation this is still not considered commercial.

Figure 4.1   Copying purpose examples   (*continued*)

Research for a commercial purpose
- Work relevant to a company's R&D.
- Work for market research or competitive intelligence in a company.
- Seeking information on a company for direct commercial ends.
- Work done by an information broker.
- Work done in drafting a book or book chapter for which authors know they are going to get royalties.
- Work done for a spin-off company or enterprise owned by a university or charity (even if all profits are covenanted to the university or charity).
- A post-doctoral research project funded by a commercial company.
- Work done to assist a private medicine service.

Figure 4.1   (*continued*)

Statutory copying and use: suggested guidance on keeping within limits

Once it has been established that copying is authorized under a permitted exception and the purpose is legitimate, users may copy for themselves or a librarian may copy for them. The following section suggests some copying limits where, up until now, there has been no challenge from rights holders, so it has been assumed that such copying is fairly 'safe' – although the recent changes mean that those copying have to be extra careful about abiding by conditions and staying within the limits. The Act is so vague that some guidance is often requested from CILIP. Also included in this section, where relevant, is guidance on the exceptions dealing with performance, e.g. performing sound recordings.

Scanning considerations

The definition of copying is regardless of the medium, so the copy could be a digitally scanned copy, a photocopy of a scanned digital copy, or a copy downloaded from the web. Also, there are additional considerations attached to scanning as works could easily be used for other unauthorized purposes, for example storing the work on a network. It is advised, therefore, that if an organization, e.g. an educational institution, is authorized under a statutory exception to scan (copy), any communal hard disk should be wiped clean periodically in case anything has been inadvertently stored as there could be a danger of the work being copied again. The other main danger is that of infringing the right of communication to the public by the inclusion of a scanned work in e-mails, discussion lists, on websites, intranets, etc. Also, altering the digital work in any way would be infringing the moral right of integrity.

Published works

Remember there are at least two copyrights in a book: the author's text and the publisher's typographical arrangement. It is safe to say that if an author is out of copyright and the work was published over 25 years ago then the whole or substantial parts of the text may be copied. Be warned, however, that there may be new works, e.g. a foreword or an introduction, which are still in copyright.

No specific amounts are given in the Act for copying under fair dealing for research for a non-commercial purpose or private study. In theory, one could copy any amount which is not a substantial part. However, this is not very helpful to information professionals in charge of the collection of copyright-protected materials and especially those on the front line responsible for giving guidance to users. Some parameters are needed.

The library exceptions in the Act state that *a reasonable proportion* from a published edition may be copied. A *fair* amount equates with a reasonable proportion, and so the same limits could be applied to the fair dealing for research for a non-commercial purpose or private study exception. The big question is, what is reasonable or fair? Although this has never been tested it is generally agreed that one complete chapter, or extracts amounting to a maximum of 5%, of a published work would be reasonable and fair, and these limits are recommended by CILIP. The CLA also follows these limits in its standard licences.

Although no amounts are given in the Act, the generally accepted limits for quotations under fair dealing for criticism or review are: one extract of no more than 400 words; several extracts, none of which is more than 300 words, totalling no more than 800 words; or up to 40 lines from a poem (this should not exceed more than one-quarter of the whole poem).

Poems, short stories and other short literary works

These are whole works in themselves and therefore should not be copied without permission, but with regard to collections or anthologies, a short story or poem of not more than 10 pages may be copied. Remember also that a poem or short story, whose author is out of copyright, contained in a collection or anthology published over 25 years ago may be copied freely, as the typographical arrangement copyright will also have expired. Poems embedded in a chapter of a book may be treated as part of the chapter.

For short books, reports or pamphlets without chapters, up to 10% of a work is reasonable, provided that the extract does not amount to more than 20 pages.

British Standards

The BSI agreed in 1989 – and confirmed subsequently with the LA (CILIP) –

that a fair amount to copy for research or private study from a British Standard is up to 10%. This amount is the same for copying from a printed Standard, microform or CD-ROM. It is recommended that, since the 2003 changes to the Act, the fair-dealing copying is for non-commercial research purposes or private study only. The BSI has licensing schemes for any multiple or 'unfair' copying. See Chapter 6, page 108.

Unpublished works

One may copy whole works if they are unpublished under fair dealing or the library and archive regulations, but only for research for a non-commercial purpose or private study.

Computer programs

The Act says that a lawful user of a computer program is allowed to make a back-up copy which may be used to replace the original if it is corrupted and the program needs to be restored, or if the software goes missing. In the case of books with accompanying software, if the software is stolen or goes missing, a lawful user may make a further copy to replace the missing disc.

Databases

The problem with deciding whether copying from databases under an exception is fair is confusing, as databases could be subject to both copyright and database regulations depending on their originality. As the exceptions under database right are more restrictive than those under copyright (fair dealing), it has been recommended by the Patent Office that it is sensible (and less confusing) to make judgements on copying using the database right exceptions only.

It is explicitly stated in the database regulations that exceptions are only given to lawful users, and a lawful user is described as any person who (whether under a licence to do any of the acts restricted by any database right or otherwise) has a right to use the database. CILIP believes that a lawful user could therefore be: any purchaser of a printed database; any purchaser of a portable database (e.g. CD-ROM); any licensed user of an electronic database; and any client of an information service or library which is a lawful user.

It is an infringement of database right if someone extracts and reutilizes a substantial part of the contents of a database without authorization. However, lawful users are allowed to extract or reutilize insubstantial parts of a database which has been made available to the public (undefined in this case) in any manner, and this may not be restricted by any contract. The term 'insubstantial' is unclear, so it is advised that copying under this exception be treated with caution, and extracts copied be limited to a few. Even a few insubstantial extracts may be seen as a substantial amount if they are systematically extracted. The case between the British Horseracing Board and William Hill rested on this term (see Chapter 7, page 135), but the judgment did not really make things any clearer. It was judged that any data that was useful was seen to be substantial. However, in this case the copying was for direct commercial purposes. If William Hill were a not-for-profit organization, there might well have been a different outcome.

Lawful users (see above) are allowed to extract *but not reutilize* a substantial amount for the purposes of illustration for teaching or non-commercial research. Illustration for teaching is undefined and so could be interpreted widely. One example could be the copying of substantial extracts from a statistical database and displaying them on a screen to a class. They must not be reutilized, however, under this exception. So unless authorization has been obtained elsewhere, e.g. under subscription contract or with permission, extracts may not be: used to compile another database intended to be available to the public; used to communicate to the public on the web; or included in handouts to any member of the public. Members of the public includes students in this case.

Yellow Pages and similar directories

Yellow Pages is an example of a database which is protected by copyright and database right. As has been seen above, it is safest and simplest to follow the exceptions under database right when allowing copying. However, several years prior to the database right changes, BT, which used to own the rights in the Yellow Pages directories, agreed with the LA that, under fair dealing for research or private study purposes, one classified section may be copied by library users, provided that the amount copied was no more than five pages, even though a classified section could be more than five pages. If a librarian did the copying for the user under the terms of the library regulations, then more could perhaps be copied.

Although Yellow Pages is now owned by Yell Ltd, there is no reason to believe that these modest agreed amounts would be challenged as anything but insubstantial. So, for example, lawful users of a public library wanting to extract and reutilize Yellow Pages data for themselves, i.e. under database right, should stick to this amount. Lawful users may extract but not reutilize substantial amounts for the purposes of illustration for teaching or research, so far more than the five pages restriction may be copied for these purposes. If copying takes place under the copyright library exceptions, librarians will be able to fulfil non-commercial research or private study requests only. Those users needing to copy more than insubstantial amounts for commercial purposes should be advised to contact the rights holders for permission. Similarly, if accessing data on the web, conditions of access and downloading must be respected.

Articles from journals or periodicals

Under the library regulations, librarians working in prescribed libraries which are not for profit are restricted to copying only one article from any periodical issue for their users. Accordingly, CILIP recommends that users making their own copies (under fair dealing for non-commercial research or private study) should not exceed the same limit.

An article is defined as 'any item'. When several small items appear together (e.g. news items without separate authors) they may be treated as one item, unless they form an unreasonable proportion of the periodical issue. For example, it would be unreasonable to expect a user to ensure that a copy was not made of several unwanted items printed on a page alongside the item that was required.

A contents page counts as one item. So, as only one article may be copied from a journal issue subject to a request under the library regulations, copying and circulating several unsolicited contents pages could be seen as copyright infringement. However, it is the view of CILIP that circulating journal contents pages is a way of advertising the journals and does not necessarily damage the economic rights of rights holders. In fact, the opposite damages economic rights: if users do not know what is in the journal, the journal is less likely to be read, and when budgets are tight these journals are more likely to be cancelled. Many publishers now agree with this view and do not see this practice as encouraging copyright infringement. Therefore, it is unlikely that rights holders would object if journal contents pages were displayed or circulated, provided it was only to a specified group of users. Many publishers and document-supply services have table of contents services available electronically. Circulating these would be subject to contract or licence.

Publisher offprints should be treated as the original work, so if the work is an article then a copy may be made under fair dealing or the library regulations.

Subject to a request and payment, a document-supply service such as the BLDSC will supply copies of articles as well as extracts from published editions. Such copies may be requested for private study or for research for a non-commercial purpose, and are supplied on the understanding that they will be used for those purposes only. Single articles may be requested to supplement the collection of a library under the library regulations (s. 41).

Sending copyright works by fax

Copying and sending a copyright work by fax has long been seen as a legal grey area. Faxing usually involves storage in an electronic form, however briefly, and often involves making an extra hard copy to use in the machine. These could be considered as 'transient or incidental to some other use of the work' (s.17 (2) and (6)) and thus an infringement of the reproduction right. However, as long as the fax transmission is performed under a legitimate copyright exception, e.g. the library and archive regulations, it is lawful and therefore there should be no infringement. Transient and incidental copying for a legitimate purpose is exempted under the new section 28A as long as the copy made has no independent economic significance. If the transmitted hard copy is destroyed, the electronic format is deleted and all the relevant copyright regulations have been complied with (the signed declaration has been obtained before copying), there should be no problem in sending a lawful copy by fax.

Artistic works

Although normally the copying of whole works should be done only if permission or licence has been granted, there is some copying of artistic works which is unlikely to harm rights holders. Fair dealing for private study or research for a non-commercial purpose is allowed, although, like all fair dealing, it is subject to the tests of fairness (see above). Copying whole artistic works means copying more than a substantial part and so could infringe, thus increasing the risks. Discretion should therefore be used.

Students could copy an artistic work for a project as long as no further copies are made without permission or licence. In any case systematic and multiple copying by or for students of artistic works is covered in the CLA licence (see Chapter 6, pages 98, 101). Project work copying could be covered by fair dealing for non-commercial research or the exception for examination purposes. Artistic works may be used in a thesis or dissertation as this copying would be covered by the examination exception (s. 32 (3)). However, if the thesis was later to be 'dealt with', i.e. sold or let for hire or offered to be sold or let for hire, or communicated to the public, then permission would be needed for those uses. For example, if the thesis were later to be published, then this would infringe unless any works copied and included were cleared for this purpose. There is a legal requirement to acknowledge any copies made under the education exceptions unless it proves impossible to do so.

For non-commercial teaching purposes in an educational establishment, a copy or an extract of an artistic work, e.g. a graph or illustration, may be copied onto an acetate, put into a PowerPoint presentation and projected to accompany a lecture (s. 32 (1)) as long as it is acknowledged. Artistic works lawfully made available to the public, e.g. downloaded from a legitimate website, may be similarly copied (s. 32 (2A)). Unless covered by a licence or otherwise authorized, copies made for this purpose should not be reproduced in a handout.

Although artistic works may not be copied under the library regulations, librarians may copy illustrations if they form part of an article from a periodical or are included in extracts from other published editions (ss. 38 (1) and 39 (1)).

Artistic works and adaptation

Artists, designers and photographers are very anxious about adaptation of their works, as artistic works may be manipulated easily while in digital format. New 'works' could be created from such manipulations without acknowledgement of the authors. For example, technology has made it easier for a pattern or design to be manipulated to the extent that it would be difficult to recognize the original work or works. Of course, whether the new works qualified for copyright protection would depend on the degree of originality.

With this in mind, manipulating such works for experimentation purposes, e.g. making a collage, within an educational or domestic environment should not harm their legitimate interests as long as any resulting work is later deleted. It would be foolish, for example, to copy an artistic work without authorization from the rights holder and to communicate it to the public on a network. It would be even more foolish to adapt it first and claim copyright in the adaptation. It would be permitted to enlarge an artistic work for a visually impaired person to be able to see detail (see Chapter 2, page 32).

Tables and graphs

Tables fall under the definition of a literary work. Graphs fall under artistic works definition. So whereas a table may be copied for a user under the library regulations, a graph may not be. However, both categories may be copied under fair dealing for research for a non-commercial purpose or private study. Data from various tables or graphs may be extracted by lawful users and used in other works as long as substantial parts of the compilation are not copied, as such extraction and reutilization would infringe database right.

Maps and plans

Ordnance Survey mapping is Crown copyright but is not subject to the waiver as described in Chapter 5, pages 80–1. OS maps over 50 years old may be copied as they are out of copyright.

One may copy maps under fair dealing, but not under the library regulations, as maps are defined as artistic works. However, the OS signed an agreement in 1993 with The Library Association, Joint Consultative Committee on Copyright (now LACA) and the British Committee for Map Information and Cataloguing Systems (BRICMICS) to allow librarians to copy OS maps for their users, subject to certain conditions. This agreement has since expired, but CILIP is negotiating with the Ordnance Survey to reach a further understanding. In the meantime, there is no reason why such copying should not continue, provided that the new restrictions on copying for commercial research and private study are recognized. Requests must be accompanied by a copyright declaration form and meet the other conditions specified in the library regulations. The maximum amount which may be copied is four copies of a single extract from an OS or OS-based map not exceeding 625 cm^2 (A4 size). These must be straight scale copies i.e. they may not be enlarged. The same amount may be copied by a person copying for themselves under fair dealing for the purposes of research for a non-commercial purpose or private study. This extends to making copies from digital mapping as well.

Under the OS Service Level Agreement for local authorities (see Chapter 6, page 112), public libraries have to be careful not to allow any copying from OS maps other than for fair-dealing purposes. Copies should not be made, under the pretence of fair dealing, for the purpose of submitting a planning application, for example. How this can be prevented is a matter of library policy, but the OS has suggested in the past that, where possible, copies should be stamped *fair dealing* so that the planning department is alerted.

Copying from other OS mapping derivative publications, such as A-Z® or Estate Publications, should remain within fair dealing limits. The OS-recommended amount does not apply to them.

Experian Goad Ltd supply their retail plans to public libraries with a licence to copy. Permission to copy is given for students only provided evidence is given, such as a student card or other acceptable form of identification, e.g. a college letterhead confirming attendance at that establishment. Goad has stipulated that copies may not be made for any other purpose. It is advised that colleges should make this arrangement and the conditions known to their students. The amount allowed to be copied is the same as from an OS map – up to four copies of a single extract not exceeding A4 (625 cm^2). Students should sign a form declaring that the copy is for research or private-study purposes only.

Book jackets, and CD and other multimedia covers

Artistic works may be displayed or exhibited without permission because this does not infringe copyright. However, this does not extend to making photocopies or scanned copies of such for display. Permission is required.

Thumbnail images

Some librarians include a thumbnail print of images in their collection to complement the bibliographic details of slide catalogues. Although this seems a perfectly reasonable practice, it is not without risk. Rights holders may need to be convinced that the thumbnail copy would not be enlarged and distributed freely. It is safest, therefore, to use low resolution images. It is allowed to make copies of artistic works when advertising them for sale. Thumbnails are usually used for this purpose.

Clip-art images may be copied freely as these are designed for this purpose.

Photographs of art works

Taking a photograph or filming a wall-mounted picture in copyright would be an infringement unless the pictures in a film are incidental, e.g. panning around the room (s. 31). In any case, taking photographs or filming in art galleries is not likely to be allowed even if the artistic works in question are out of copyright. Although in theory these works are out of copyright and in the public domain and could be copied, owners of galleries may prevent photography on their premises. This is their right to control access, not copyright. If an artistic work in the public domain, e.g. a Turner landscape, is photographed there could be a new copyright in the photograph if there was enough skill in the production to fulfil the originality criterion. However, since the Bridgeman v. Corel case, there is some doubt about this (see Chapter 7, page 129).

Microforms

Microforms which reproduce an original work without amendment (for example, a microfilmed report) should be treated in the same way as the original. The microform is a copyright photograph but with only a facsimile copy of works on it, and copies have no copyright in themselves. A microform publisher might own additional rights as editor or compiler of an anthology, in which case permission to copy may be necessary. Otherwise only the rights of the authors and publishers of the original works apply to ordinary sized copying.

Printed music

Suppliers of printed music, including digital sheet music, have a very limited customer base as only those who can read music will purchase. Therefore, any copyright infringement of printed music will damage their industry more than infringements in the book publishing industry. CILIP advocates following the Music Publishers Association (MPA) Code of Fair Practice agreed between composers and publishers of printed music (see Chapter 10, page 170). This guidance booklet sets out what the safe limits are for copying under the exceptions and gives guidance for copying in other specific circumstances.

The fair dealing exception for copying for non-commercial research or private study applies to printed music. Librarians may also make and supply a copy of a part of a musical work under the library regulations for the same purposes. In order to encourage compliance, it would be preferable not to allow any self-copying of sheet music but instead to supply copies to users under the library regulations in accordance with the MPA Code. This way one can ensure the Code is followed. It is for the requester to decide what is a reasonable and fair amount to copy. It is difficult to specify limits as each case is likely to be different. The test for fair dealing should be applied when in doubt (see above).

The Code, available free from the MPA and at the time of writing under revision following the recent changes, also outlines other permissions to copy for specific circumstances. For education uses, the Code states that 'Bona fide students or teachers, whether they are in an educational establishment or not, may without application to the copyright owner make copies of short excerpts of musical works provided that they are for study only (not for performance). Copying whole movements or whole works is expressly forbidden under this permission.' If the copying is for examination purposes, printed music may be copied as well as any other material. However, students being examined for their music performance may not use photocopied music. Items needed for this purpose must be purchased as this exception expressly forbids making copies for performance purposes.

Sound recordings, films and broadcasts

There is no provision in the Act for making back-up copies of commercially produced sound recordings or videos. A damaged cassette or video tape beyond repair which is still required would have to be discarded and another purchased.

Fair dealing for the purposes of non-commercial research or private study does not apply to sound recordings, films or broadcasts. Similarly, librarians may not copy these categories for a user under the library regulations. Although it is a common practice by the general public, one may *not* copy a sound recording to give to a friend, to put into a different format, e.g. from a CD to a cassette, to make a compilation of several different recordings. It is also illegal to download (or upload) sound recordings and films from and to the web unless authorized.

One may copy a sound recording, film or broadcast which has been made available to the public for the purposes of fair dealing for criticism or review as long as the sound recording, film or broadcast is acknowledged. Fair dealing for reporting current events also applies. Again there is a requirement to acknowledge. However, no acknowledgement is required where this would be impossible for reasons of practicality or otherwise.

In education, copying for the purposes of examination and copying films and sound recordings for the purposes of teaching film and sound-recording production is permitted. No limits are given for such copying. Remember that if any copies are subsequently dealt with, these become infringing. Educational establishments are allowed to record broadcasts off-air and use them within the establishment for educational purposes unless there is a licensing scheme available. There are two: ERA and the Open University schemes. See Chapter 6, pages 113–15 for details.

Performance

Showing a film or broadcast or playing a sound recording *in public* is not covered by any exception. Such performance must be covered by a licence (see Chapter 6, pages 115–16). So if a public library wished to play background music or show a video, both acts would have to be licensed. Students and teachers in an educational establishment are not seen as the public in this case so it is permitted to show films and play sound recordings to them but not to parents or any other audience.

Clubs, societies and other organizations may play sound recordings as part of their activities, or for their benefit, as long as such organizations are not run for profit and their main objects are charitable or concerned with the advancement of religion, education or social welfare (s. 67) (see Chapter 2, page 35). In any organized event, no profit must be made, so any charge for admission must cover only operating expenses. This includes anyone involved with the event who makes any money, e.g. disc jockeys. So, to give an example, if a school or student union wished to hold a disco in order to raise funds, the playing of sound recordings would need to be authorized by licence. Whereas if the local opera appreciation society planned to play recordings of some Verdi arias at an organized event and the society was not intending to raise funds, as the admission charge would cover only costs (and no one would be paid for any service), this would not need to be licensed as it would be permitted by the exception. Libraries are not clubs or societies so any playing of a sound recording in a public library would need to be licensed. For example, the playing of a story cassette to a group of children, or background music in the library, would need licences from both the Performing Right Society and Phonographic Performance Ltd. See details of the PRS and PPL in Chapter 6, pages 115–16.

The web/internet

Provided they meet the criteria for protection, works which appear on the internet are someone's intellectual property. Many believe that material on the internet is copyright free. This is not so. All the rules of copyright which apply to printed material also apply to works in digital form. Collections of documents on websites are clearly databases and all the rules regarding databases apply. What appears sometimes to be free from copyright restrictions may just be copyright waived. Some works have notices to this effect. A lot of the content on the internet is there for the express purpose of its being read, copied, or downloaded. Some of it is ephemeral. Some material may even consist of infringing copies. It is difficult for some content providers to control copying and reuse of their material, but if material is difficult to access and copy – for example, it is accessed via a password – it is clear that such content providers are not waiving their copyright, and so conditions of use should be respected. Similarly, by reading conditions of access on-screen, and clicking to say that these are understood and accepted, means one has entered into a form of contract. The option is always there of negotiating with content providers for uses over and above these terms (see Chapter 5, pages 74–8). If there is a helpful notice on material which allows more copying and use than (normally allowed) under statute, then copying may take place within these limits. If there is no explicit copyright notice on a website, there may be an implicit licence to copy. Discretion should be used, of course, especially with commercial reuse, and if in doubt users should be encouraged to stick to the generally agreed amounts for copying from printed works. One must always keep the test of fairness in mind and whether the purpose of copying is covered by a statutory authorization.

Statutory exceptions do apply to the internet so, for example, if a literary, dramatic, musical or artistic item from a website is required for research for a non-commercial purpose or private study, for criticism or review, or for teaching, etc., then one may download it for these purposes. What one may do with the downloaded item must also be considered, as a work in electronic format can easily be moved around networks, can easily be copied several times and also can easily be plagiarized. Downloading to print should be fine. Downloading to a PC for long-term consultation should also be acceptable as long as the PC is not networked. Downloading to a networked PC or to an intranet would not be acceptable as the item potentially would be available for many to see and so would likely be an infringement of the author's communication to the public right. In any case, if the work was on a publicly available network, i.e. one that has not been accessed under contractual terms, then there would be no reason to place the item on an intranet as a link to the site would be all that was required. Downloading items from websites accessed under contractual terms will be dealt with in Chapter 5, pages 83–4.

Creating web pages, intranets and VLEs

Unless explicitly authorized, copyrighted protected works – whether digitally scanned under statute or under licence, or born digital – should never be included on an electronic network which is available to the public, as this infringes the right of communication to the public. It is important this is understood, as such copies are visible and so risks are a lot higher: it will be easier for the author to take action, and it could be judged a criminal offence. The meaning of 'public' is likely to be anything outside the domestic circle, and so very broad. Intranets and virtual learning environments are regarded as public networks too. Permission or licence must be obtained.

Any content placed on a website or network should, therefore, either be owned entirely by the organization concerned or be cleared by obtaining permission to use (see Chapter 5, pages 71–4). The copyright in an actual website (which is in effect a database), regardless of content, is owned by its maker. Copyright holders are entitled to prevent unauthorized copying from their sites and many are beginning to use technical means to prevent access copying. At present it would be foolish for information professionals to put unprotected copyright works onto a website if they did not want them copied at all. In any case, recognizing the restricted copying allowed under a statutory exception is good public relations. It is suggested that a helpful copyright notice such as the one given in Figure 5.2, page 84, be placed somewhere on a website homepage indicating what may be copied and for what purposes.

Some basic points to note:

- make sure that all content on the website has been cleared for inclusion
- if the site is being developed by someone else, make sure that all the relevant authorizations (assignments or licences of copyright works) are obtained from the developer before the site goes live
- ensure that any regular contributors are aware of the risks of website publication and dangers of infringement, and obtain, preferably in writing, an agreement with all contributors to include assurances and indemnities to protect your organization against possible claims for copyright infringement.

Linking and framing

Although failure to do so is not prevented by law, it has always been good practice to ask permission to include links to other websites and to review such links on a regular basis in case they are no longer valid. The link should ideally be to the home page of the other website.

With regard to including links to external websites which seek to bypass a homepage (deep linking), a pragmatic approach can be taken, bearing in mind that legal experts are predicting that there may be legal restrictions in the pipeline. There have been many test cases but at present these seem to be contradicting each other, so it is still unclear as to whether this is an infringement of copyright (and maybe database right) or not (see Chapter 7, pages 132–3). It may depend on what one is linking to. If an organization links to articles and data on a rival website without asking permission, this may be challenged (as has happened – see pages 132–3), but on the other hand there may be no objection to a deep link to relevant information on another site provided it is made clear on the host site that one is leaving one site and entering another. Alerting others to an item on a website by email is acceptable.

Framing, whereby images from another website are displayed on an organization's website within frames containing its own material, would almost certainly need permission as it is tantamount to including the work on the home website.

E-mail messages and discussion lists

Many assume that e-mail recipients may use messages freely. However, the copyright in e-mails, like letters, belongs to the author (or the employer if created as part of the employment contract). Permission to copy and use is often implied and understood, so to keep e-mails personal and confidential, a notice to that effect should be included in the message. Sending a message to a public discussion list is like sending a letter to the editor of a newsletter, i.e. an implied licence is given to share the contents with subscribers unless there was clear evidence to the contrary. The copyright in the message still belongs to the sender even though it may be forwarded to other lists, quoted and archived. Moral rights also apply, so a message should never be quoted without being acknowledged; it should not be attributed to someone else; nor should it be manipulated or treated in a derogatory fashion. Messages sent to a closed list should not be forwarded to a public list without asking the sender's permission. All copyright notices attached to e-mails should be respected.

Local studies material

It is important that the copyright status of material in local studies collections or archives is known as this helps with later requests for copies. What material is in copyright? What material is in the public domain? Has the material ever been published? Who owns the copyright? If it is unpublished, has permission been given to copy it? Is it subject to publication right? (see Chapter 1, pages 13–14). If the material is still in copyright, all copying and use must be in accordance with permitted exceptions, i.e. either copied by the library staff under the library regulations, or copied under fair dealing. Broadcasting or communicating material to the public on a website needs permission.

Local studies material, especially photographic material, is a valuable resource and it is often sought after for commercial exploitation, e.g. for publishing in a book or on a web page. The library or archive must be clear about sanctioning such use, and guidance should ideally be included in a library copyright policy. Unless copyright has been assigned to the library or archive, the only person who could authorize such copying would be the rights holder or their estate. Library staff should not assume that just because they hold the original, that they also hold the copyright. Neither should it be assumed that donations from members of the public include assignment of copyright. Cases have been reported where a local member of the public has seen his photographs donated to the public library turned into postcards and sold in local shops; another set of photographs turned up in a local publication without permission or even any acknowledgement. In such cases rights holders are completely justified in making complaints to the library or even to sue for infringement.

When the material is part of a donation and the identity of the rights holders is unknown, if it can be reasonably assumed that the material is out of copyright or the rights holder has waived copyright, then copying may take place. However, if there is uncertainty, it may be that there is a higher than normal risk of infringement, and so legal advice should be sought.

Here are some practical suggestions:

- Where possible, establish the copyright status of existing material and whether it has ever been published. For example, if a work has never been published it is probably still in copyright until 2039 – see the library regulation on copying unpublished works in Chapter 2, page 25, and the section on unpublished works in Chapter 1, page 10.
- Before accepting donations, establish the copyright and published status.
- Keep a record of who donated what and the conditions of further copying. This is essential anyway for unpublished works. Does the author mind the work being copied and used? What about commercial use? Does the library itself have permission to exploit it, or put it on a publicly accessible website, e.g. the People's Network?
- If necessary, involve lawyers in drawing up a contract stating all the terms.
- When tracing copyright holders, make every reasonable attempt. If this proves unsuccessful, insist that copying may only be for research for a non-commercial purpose or private study (use the declaration forms) or make it clear to any would-be exploiters the status of the material and that the onus is on them if they use it for a commercial purpose. However, the latter is not

foolproof. Rights holders may place blame on the library or archive for allowing the material to be exploited.
• Seek legal advice if at all unsure.

Networking local studies material is more complicated and there are many issues to consider. A relevant question is included in Chapter 9, pages 161–3.

Miscellaneous advice and guidance

The following section covers the copying and use of material not falling into one of the specific categories described above or which deserves special consideration.

Advertisements

One might assume that copying advertisements, especially in education, would be acceptable. Even though they are still protected by copyright, advertisers would want them to be spread around non-conventional channels. However, advertisements, even printed ones, can have complicated rights clearance issues, including product design rights (see Chapter 1, page 15), and so it is not advisable to copy them other than for private study. They are excluded from the DACS slide licensing scheme for this reason (see Chapter 6, pages 108–9).

Committee papers

It seems clear that multiple copies made for a committee for consideration at a meeting may not be regarded as fair dealing for 'research for a non-commercial purpose'. 'Private study' is clearly not applicable in the case of committees. It has been argued that 'criticism or review' is an appropriate purpose for committees. Multiple copies are allowed for this fair-dealing purpose. For consultative documents, it is in the interests of those publishers and rights holders that other organizations consider and respond to them.

The following 'rules of thumb' are offered to assist in preparing committee papers:

• *Circular letters and similar documents seeking the views of individuals and organizations*: it may be assumed that copies may be made without permission.
• *Unpriced consultative documents*: if an unpriced document is labelled 'consultative' or similar, it may be assumed that the publisher wishes it to be widely circulated in order to receive comments. In most cases, it will probably be acceptable to copy for committees. Free additional copies may be easily available from the publisher, in which case this may be the preferred option.

- *Priced consultative documents*: it would be wise to obtain permission to copy either an extract or the whole document. An extract worth copying for a committee, e.g. the conclusions and recommendations, could be considered a 'substantial' part.
- *Crown and Parliamentary publications*: if these are available on a Government department website and do not have any copying restriction notice attached to them, then these may be copied freely, subject to the HMSO conditions of copying (see Chapter 5, pages 80–3). Legislative and other material subject to the waiver may also be copied freely, subject to the HMSO conditions of copying.
- *All other priced publications (including HMSO material)*: it is advisable to obtain permission from the publishers.

Many publishers may freely give permission to copy for committee purposes, if asked. All copies made for a committee should have a full bibliographical reference, the source of 'official' copies, and should be marked 'for committee consideration only'. It cannot be assumed that committee members may make further copies to circulate in their workplace, for example. Unless specific permission has been obtained, it is advisable not to include copies of copyright documents with sets of committee papers which are sent to other people for information only. Sources of supply of the original documents may instead be included on agendas, or digests could be prepared. Establishments covered by a licence may copy copyright material covered by that licence for use by a committee within the limits of the licence.

Company reports

Annual reports are protected by copyright as they are original literary works and so are subject to the same restrictions. However, this kind of material is often copyright-waived in that one can copy freely from it. It is advised that the material should not be used to damage or prejudice the economic interests of the rights holders. It is likely to be acceptable to use scanned images from a few pages of the annual reports of several major companies for use in an internal database. However, it would be an infringement if substantial amounts were collected from annual reports for a commercial exploitation purpose without the rights holders' permission. Company reports issued on microfiche by Companies House may be treated in the same way as the originals. However, Companies House will have database right with regard to the unfair extraction and reutilization of the contents, so the copying of a substantial part of the microfiche, especially for a commercial purpose, would need to be cleared with Companies House.

Copyright-cleared workbooks in schools

Some publishers allow the free copying of these school workbooks and they are supplied for this purpose. The price of copying is incorporated into the purchase price. However, copies should be used only by staff and students within the establishment, as it would be unfair to borrow a copy from another library to take advantage of the copyright-waived material.

Copying by students in public libraries

Many public libraries are frequently used by students doing research for project work as they may be more convenient than using their own academic libraries for various reasons – under-resourced school libraries, the school library being unavailable after school, etc. The CLA multiple-copying licence does not extend to public libraries, and so any copying in public libraries is restricted to the permitted statutory exceptions. Therefore, the public library has to cope with the challenge of balancing the educational needs of students with the need to respect copyright by working within the spirit of fair dealing and the require-ments of the library regulations. CILIP advises that, where necessary, public libraries and educational establishments co-operate on the provision of photo-copies of material for group projects. Individual students may still copy for their own non-commercial research and private study under fair dealing subject to the restrictions, and provided the copying falls within the conditions of the library regulations, librarians may copy on their behalf.

Current awareness bulletins and document supply

Anyone may produce an in-house current awareness bulletin if the biblio-graphic details have been input manually, i.e. not obtained by photocopying contents pages or downloading from an online database (although this may be possible if licensed or with permission). Annotations and abstracts may be included, and section 60 allows any abstracts published along with articles in scientific or technical journals to be incorporated in a current awareness bul-letin. The interpretation of 'scientific' or 'technical' may be assumed to be broad to include the humanities. It would be an infringement to make multiple copies of relevant journal articles as part of a selective dissemination of information (SDI) service and disseminate them to users.

Sections 38, 39 and 43 of the Act clearly authorize prescribed non-profit-based libraries to provide a copying service for the purposes of research for a non-commercial purpose or private study, in response to requests. However, any library which advertised a copying service in direct association with a bulletin, especially if distributed beyond the normal clientele or catchment area, could be considered to be soliciting requests rather than responding to them, which would be in breach of the regulations. Also such services could be seen to be competing with other commercial document supply services. Therefore, CILIP recommends that any library sending bulletin copies outside the institution should encourage recipients, where possible, to obtain photocopies of items from a local source.

It is also preferable to include standard declaration forms only in issues distributed to the library's own clientele. If forms are included in all copies it should be made clear that they are for use only by registered members in the relevant catchment area or by the 'closed' clientele.

Electoral registers in public libraries

The Representation of the People Act 2000, which came into effect in October 2002, has affected changes to how the Register of Electors is made available to the public. Since the changes to data privacy, following the Data Protection Act 1998, data subjects have to give their consent to their data being processed. A very significant court case between a Mr Robertson and Wakefield Council highlighted the problem of registers being sold to commercial companies that use the personal data for direct marketing purposes (see Chapter 7, page 134). The ruling has had implications for electoral registration officers (EROs), who were advised that the full electoral registers should cease to be sold to such companies. To get round the data subject consent, there are now two registers: the full version and an edited version. Members of the public may elect not to appear on the edited register.

The new rules affect the making available of the full registers in public libraries for inspection and consultation. Although it will depend on the policy of individual EROs, in theory there is nothing to prevent this practice continuing. However, as the judge in the court case stated, EROs must also consider and anticipate the purposes for which personal data are intended to be processed. This has implications, even for the consultation of the registers, if any substantial copying is allowed to take place. If commercial data collection companies are allowed to access and copy the data in the public library for free, then EROs are likely to be forced to clamp down on this as well. Therefore *all* photocopying of registers, not just those following the RPA 2000 changes, will be banned. If registers are deposited in public libraries, copying from the full registers is restricted to making brief manuscript notes, but this has to be under some degree of supervision. If local councils do not consider that their libraries can offer such safeguards, it is likely that registers may be viewable at the Electoral Registration Office only. Archive copies of superseded full registers also fall under these restrictions, which creates problems for access for genuine not-for-profit researchers. CILIP is actively trying to change this situation.

Foreign material

All material from countries party to the Berne Convention (see Chapter 8, pages 138–40) should be given the same protection (national treatment) as UK material. Similarly, UK works are protected under the copyright laws of other Berne member states. However, the extension of the term of protection in EU member states for literary, dramatic, musical and artistic works to life plus 50 to 70 years has meant that some non EEA-material will only be protected for the Berne minimum of 50 years following the end of the year of death of the author. Some works in France have an extra nine years' protection to compensate authors for the period lost in the two World Wars. The UK does not recognize this extra term, so French works in the UK have the same protection as other EEA member states. The USA has extended its term to life plus 70 years for personal authors, but corporate authors, e.g. Disney, are entitled to 95 years' protection (see Chapter 8, page 150).

Free material

Material which is circulated free of charge – brochures, press releases, leaflets, etc. – is still protected by copyright, although the copyright may be waived. It is advised that multiple copying should be with permission or further copies should be obtained. Permission would also be required for commercial exploitation.

Knitting patterns

Strictly speaking, knitting patterns are whole works and as such should not be copied. However, one can copy for research (for a non-commercial purpose) or private study, and there is no point in copying just a small part of a knitting pattern. There was a case in 1980 (*Roberts* v. *Candiware Ltd*, 1980) where it was judged that knitting patterns carry with them the implied right to reproduce the pattern for domestic purposes. Before copying, it should be ascertained if the pattern is still available commercially. If the pattern was falling apart, it could be copied under the library regulations (s. 42). Librarians are allowed to copy works for preservation purposes as long as they are not available for purchase and the copies are kept for reference.

Translations

Translating, i.e. making an adaptation, of a whole work without authorization would be an infringing act. Before translating any copyright work, therefore, the copyright holder should be consulted. This is not only because of the requirement for permission but also because of the author's moral rights which imply that the author should be made aware of a risk of misinterpretation. If permission is granted, then the copyright in the new work belongs to the translator, although the original copyright stays with the author. Translating extracts of a work for a non-commercial research purpose, private study or any of the other statutory exceptions would not normally require permission.

Training courses

If articles or extracts from published works are needed for distribution to delegates on a conference or course of training, they should be copied only with permission. Although there is an exception given in the Act for copying for an educational purpose, this is only valid if there is no licensing scheme available. As there is a licensing scheme available from the Copyright Licensing Agency, such photocopying should be covered by a CLA licence, or permission should be obtained from each publisher. Any commercially produced training videos or manuals should never be reproduced without permission.

Ten things to remember from this chapter

- when copying, one must be authorized either by statute, permission or licence
- the responsibility for copying lies with the person wishing to make the copy
- information professionals should not quiz requesters on the purpose of their copying
- whether copying is fair dealing depends on the purpose of copying at the time
- copies may be supplied by fax if the copying is legitimate
- copying from the web is permitted under fair dealing
- putting a downloaded copy on a network is not fair dealing
- be wary of deep linking without permission
- e-mails are like letters: the copyright belongs to the authors
- local studies librarians should establish the copyright and published status of donations before accepting them.

5 Copyright compliance: contractual solutions

In this chapter you will learn about:

- obtaining permission and clearing rights to use copyright material
- a basic understanding of the law of contracts and licences
- tips on negotiating licences
- copyright waivers
- web contracts.

The previous chapter dealt with copying authorized by statute. What happens when the copying in an organization is not covered by an exception? How does one copy copyright material without being accused of infringement?

The first step should be to assess the situation and think about seeking authorization from the rights holder(s) either by direct permission or a licensing solution. This chapter deals with the principles of contracts and licensing, and the types of contract, and includes suggested guidance on the process of clearing rights and negotiating licences and contracts. In the following chapter, some of the actual licences and licensing schemes will be outlined. Also included in this chapter are: details of copyright waivers where permission is given to copy freely, subject to some conditions, and some guidance on web contracts.

The need to clear rights

In the commercial world of book and media publishing, clearing rights is commonplace. No publisher will publish a work until all the necessary rights have been cleared with the authors and other rights holders. The transfer of these economic rights is normally done under contract, and there are specific guides to such contracts available for publishers to crib from.

Librarians are also having to clear rights, not always in order to exploit them commercially, though this is happening too, but mainly because statutory exceptions do not offer enough protection for the copying and planned uses of the material in question. For example, a public library holds a collection of old photographs of local interest which have been donated to them over the years, and the library wishes to digitize them and put them on to a publicly accessible website. The library cannot rely on fair dealing or any of the other exceptions, so the necessary rights (reproduction and communication to the public) in the photographs have to be cleared first. In education the reproduction right needs to be cleared to copy works not covered by fair dealing or the educational exceptions and which fall outside licensing schemes, e.g. excluded works from the CLA repertoire. In industry and commerce, where there are even fewer applicable statutory exceptions to rely on, contracting for access to information products is the norm.

Clearing rights in works

When clearing individual rights, obviously the holders of the copyrights have to be approached and permission, preferably in writing, must be obtained. Permission could be a letter or a licence/contract to use. It will depend mainly on the economic value of the material, the purpose of copying and whether rights holders are in the business of exploiting their material or not. For educational or non-commercial purposes, reactions to requests will be varied: some rights holders will be pleased just to be acknowledged and will willingly grant permission without charge; some may charge a nominal fee; some may not even have a procedure for handling such requests and so take time to reply while they are making up their minds; and some may not even realize they have rights at all! For more commercial uses, payment will obviously be required and specific conditions of use will be outlined. This is likely to be covered in a contract.

One must never underestimate the difficulties of identifying and tracing rights holders. The owner of the copyright could be: the original author if the work has never been published, or if copyright has reverted to them; the author's estate if the author is dead; the author's agent; or the publisher, if the work has been published within the last 25 years or if the work has been completely assigned.

With published works, it is advisable to begin with the publisher. If a publisher no longer owns the rights, or no longer exists, then one has to try tracing the principal author, etc. The Society of Authors may be able to help (for contact details see Appendix C). With photographs, there may be some information on the back of the photograph about the photographer. If the photographer is no longer in business, the collection may have been taken over by a picture library or archive. Tracing the photographer may prove difficult if there is no indication anywhere of the provenance of the work. In these cases, using the works is a matter of risk management.

For unpublished works, it is probably safe to say that if the author has been dead for more than 50 years and the work is over 100 years old, copying may take place as the risk of infringement is negligible. Note, however, that most unpublished works, e.g. photographs, will still be in copyright until at least 2039.

A suggested text for a letter is given in Figure 5.1. Note that it is not a good idea to add words to the effect that if they do not reply by a certain date then there is an assumption that permission is given. Permission should be explicit. If a rights holder fails to reply after several attempts to contact them, then whether the work is copied should depend on the policy of the organization. The decision to take risks should be with the full knowledge and support of management.

If it proves impossible to trace the rights holder but it is reasonable to assume the copyright has expired or that the author or authors died over 70 years ago, and there is evidence that reasonable enquiry has been made, copying could take place (s. 57). What constitutes *reasonable enquiry* would have to be decided in a court of law if the rightful owner chose to prosecute. The standards of conduct expected by the law for information professionals are likely to be higher than for the ordinary member of the public, as conducting searches is part of the business of an information professional.

Accordingly, in ascertaining whether or not a work is truly anonymous or pseudonymous, whether copyright has expired, or whether the author of the work is alive or dead, information professionals would be expected to be aware of and make full use of all sources of information appropriate to the nature of the rights required. Enquiries should be tempered by economic realities, and should be measured against the expected or probable value of the use envisaged by the person or organization wishing to make use of a work of undetermined copyright status. For example, if the copy is required for private study (assuming it is a substantial part and so not likely to be fair) then an effort should be made to trace the rights holder. In contrast, a library planning to make postcards of photographs in their collection in order to sell them would have to go to far greater lengths in their enquiry.

All steps taken in the enquiry should be recorded. Prosecutions for infringement can take place up to six years after the year of an alleged offence, so records of steps taken should ideally be kept for seven years.

If it is not reasonable to assume that a work is out of copyright but the quest for the rights holder proves elusive, there is obviously a higher risk in copying the work. If a decision is made to take a risk and use the work, it is advisable to put a notice in the publication, in the press or on a website, whatever is applicable, to say that despite all attempts it has been impossible to trace the rightful owner. One can then invite the rights holder to make contact. If the rights holder then makes themselves known and can prove that the work is rightfully theirs, this could just be a matter of a retrospective permission and perhaps payment. Provided all these steps are taken, it is unlikely that there would be a prosecution for infringement.

(Please adapt for your own circumstances. Words in italics are for guidance only)

Dear ....[*publisher/author/producer/website owner, etc.*]

[*What is to be copied?*]
I am writing to request permission or licence to reproduce and use
.... [*give details: e.g. pages X–X, chapter X, image X, article X, extract X, etc.) from (give full details: e.g. publication/work/website, etc.)*]
....
in ....
[*give full details of where item etc. is to be included: e.g. a commercial publication, on the organization website, on the organization intranet, etc.*]

[*Subsequent uses: if the work is not for commercial exploitation*]
The *publication/work/item* is not intended for commercial exploitation but is intended to be freely distributed and made available for UK educational purposes, *or*
The *publication/work/item* will be made available for non-commercial research or private-study purposes on our internal network only, *or*
The *publication/work/item* will be made available for non-commercial research or private-study purposes on our website.

[*Subsequent uses: if the work is intended for commercial publication*]
The publication will be available for sale and distributed in the *UK only/Europe/worldwide.*

It is estimated that there will be a print run of .... copies. [*necessary if a publication, commercial or otherwise*]

We would be very grateful if you could grant us permission *and give an indication of costs* [*omit if reproduction is for a non-commercial purpose*]. If you do not have the necessary rights, please indicate who could give permission.
   I look forward to an early reply. [*If you have a deadline, say so here*]

Yours sincerely

etc.

Figure 5.1   Suggested standard text for permission seeking

Some information professionals rely on a rule that says that if a published work is over 120 years old then it is more likely than not to be out of copyright. If uses are for non-commercial purposes and so lower risk, then this rule of thumb could be useful. However, an effort should be made to clear rights using the proper channels for other high-risk uses.

Contracts and licences

There are several types of licence familiar to information professionals which deal with permissions to copy and use copyright works. There is the licence which allows multiple copying of print-based materials in the licence repertoire, e.g. a CLA licence, where payment is on a one-off annual basis; there is the CLA digitization licence, which permits the scanning of print-based works where payment is usually transactional; and a licence to use a variety of born-digital works under subscription contract, e.g. journal databases.

On behalf of their users, information professionals subscribe to very many electronic publications, all of which have specific and detailed contractual terms and conditions which should define and determine access and use. These are usually written in extremely small print and often in legal jargon but, nevertheless, it is very important to read and be aware of these conditions and to understand what exactly one is agreeing to. For example, who are the authorized users and what are the authorized uses? If terms and conditions are not as expected then it may be too late to negotiate. Before entering into an agreement, therefore, it is necessary to take steps to avoid any potential pitfalls.

A licence is a contract. Contracts are agreements usually between two parties and preferably should be negotiable. To put it simply, A holds the rights to use the material. B wants to use the material. B sits down with A and discusses terms. B pays A money and A gives B permission. Obviously it is rather more complicated but these are the basic principles. Most contracts are drawn up by lawyers and sometimes the language can be confusing and off-putting. Nevertheless, it is important to understand what exactly is being agreed.

Negotiating contracts and licences

Unless the library is experienced and confident in this area, it makes sense to involve legal experts when negotiating, especially with any collective licensing scheme such as those run by the CLA or NLA. Librarians understand information; lawyers understand contracts.

The need for a licence

It may sound an obvious question but nevertheless one needs to ask why the library needs a licence, as this will influence thinking prior to negotiating. A licence may be needed for several reasons. Depending on the purpose and on what the product is, some of these reasons could be: to allow access for staff to the journals included on this database; to be able to supply copies of documents to supply to clients; to be able to make multiple copies of licensed material; to provide an indemnity for the library because fair dealing is becoming too risky (or no longer allowed by law), etc.

Consortia licensing

If possible, it also makes sense to ally with other libraries to form a consortium or umbrella body. This is useful when dealing with the licences to use born-digital material or multiple copying of print-based material. A simple example of a consortium is Universities UK which acts on behalf of all UK higher education institutions to get a good licensing deal.

Consortia licensing is being seen by many librarians, mainly in the higher education sector, as the answer to the might of publishers. The growth of bilateral agreements between publishers and academic librarians has led to a multiplicity of complex and varied conditions, not all of which are easily comprehended or digested by busy library staff. Some librarians have better deals than others. Many have been more concerned with their budgets than worrying about what a licence allowed. It was realized by some librarians that they could be in a better position to improve these deals with publishers if they pooled information and knowledge and formed library consortia. Currently around 150 national consortia groups have joined forces to become the International Coalition of Library Consortia (ICOLC). The aim of ICOLC is to share licensing information and facilitate discussion on issues of common interest. For further information see their website (details are given in Appendix C).

Authorized users

From the information professional's point of view, a simple licence which can cope with a multiplicity of users and which will give equal access to all is the ideal aim. However, from the perspective of the vendor (or representatives of the vendor), a well-defined set of users is essential. The outcome is likely to be based on costs. The fees paid are usually based on the number of staff having access, and so if budgets are tight, it is to the library's advantage to be more specific, although it is important that all those who will need to use the materials/product are covered. It could be very expensive to add a set of users later.

- Authorized users could be all the staff in an organization, including those on other sites in the UK and abroad. Should affiliated companies be included?
- Authorized users could be restricted to certain categories of staff. For example, some licences specify professional employees who are usually those on a certain grade and above. This would cut out the junior and ancillary staff.
- If the library/organization is open to the public, should the licence cover walk-in users as well?
- In education, do distance learners in the UK and abroad need access?

Cheaper deals?

Negotiating contracts and licences should be about obtaining the most suitable terms and conditions for your library users. It should not just be about obtaining the cheapest deal to use the material. A cheaper deal can mean more restrictive terms and conditions. Once signed, parties have to abide by the terms and conditions, so it is important to get them right first time and not when renewal is up in three years. A cheap deal can be more expensive in the long run as much administrative time can be spent by staff sorting out the problems caused by the restrictions.

Contract v. statute law

Contract law can override statute (i.e. copyright) law, although ideally it should not. UK copyright law is designed to provide a careful balance between protecting copyright works from unfair use and abuse and allowing access for lawful public-interest purposes. Any contract which tries to take away or limit a statutory permission is therefore upsetting this balance and should be avoided. It would be foolish, for example, to accept a condition which prevented a user from downloading a copy to use for research purposes. It is debatable, in any case, whether such contracts which attempt to limit fair practices are valid. Any clause to that effect could be challenged as unfair. However, it is highly unlikely that an information professional would dare or even wish to make such a challenge without legal help. It is better to ensure, therefore, that any contract signed by the library does not limit an exception. *Buying into a contract or licence should extend what one can do under statute, not reduce it.*

Parties bound by contract

Only the parties signing the licence are bound by its terms. It would not be appropriate to ask individual users to agree to the terms in any separate contract. For example, a university should not ask students to sign (or click to agree) before using any of the licensed material, even though the university may be bound to make students comply with the terms.

Access required?

Before entering into any contract, agreement or licence, it is necessary to establish what access is needed, who needs access and for what purposes it is needed. It is always important to establish what one can do with any information product, preferably before purchase. If the product is not fit for the purpose for which it is intended, one should be able to negotiate terms or decide not to buy. This may not be so easy with an 'off the peg' licensing scheme where there may not be much room to alter the basic licence terms.

Material to be covered by the licence

Is this going to be a true blanket licence i.e. covering all material in the collection, or are there excluded works and categories? If it is a digitization licence, how comprehensive is it? For example, is the licence limited to scanning UK material only or are foreign materials included?

If the licence does not cover the material in your collection, further permission may have to be obtained directly from rights holders. This could prove difficult especially if such works are foreign or obscure. The CLA, for example, does not have reciprocal agreements with all countries and so is unable to indemnify some foreign works against accusations of copyright infringement. Is the licence worth having if it is not fit for the purpose?

What are the authorized uses?

With a negotiated licence, one should be able, rights holders permitting, to customize uses and terms to suit the purpose. Consider what staff and/or users would like to do (or are already doing!) and this should govern what needs to be covered by a licence. Depending on the type of authorization needed, some likely uses could be:

- downloading items to a personal computer for temporary storage
- scanning items and sending them to clients electronically by e-mail or fax
- including printed copies or extracts of items in written presentations for clients
- including extracts of items in training presentations (e.g. PowerPoint) to staff or clients
- including items in handouts

- multiple copying of licensed material for students:
  — on campus
  — off campus, i.e. distance learning.

Although a specific use is unlikely to be spelt out, it should not be excluded either if it is what is needed by an organization.

Shrink-wrap and online end-user licences

Not all contracts are negotiable. For example, licences, familiarly called shrink-wrap because they are completely encased in a cling film, which accompany software are purchased on a take it or leave it principle: if one buys the product and unwraps it, one is bound by the licence terms. If one does not agree to the licence terms, then the product may be returned to the vendor. Similarly, online access to certain websites is governed by the user agreeing up front to abide by the terms and conditions. If the user does not click to agree, then further access is denied. There is no other legal way of accessing the contents of such sites. Such non-negotiated licences are believed to be enforceable.

Implied contracts and prohibitive statements

Some publications, such as market research reports, contain statements which seem to forbid any copying. By purchasing them for the library, it could be said that information professionals had entered into an 'implied contract' with the publishers. Where copying is permitted by the Act (e.g. under fair dealing or the library regulations) or under a licence, it is most unlikely that a rights holder would bring a claim of infringement of 'implied contract' to court because of some phrase which had been put on an item. The law on unfair contract terms could be used in defence in any case, should a need arise. In general, therefore, it is advised that such prohibitive or restrictive phrases, which appear to limit copying or use of an item to a greater extent than statute, may be ignored. It is a different case if conditions of sale were agreed prior to purchase or a full contract were entered into, as then a rights holder would be entitled to enforce conditions. Contract law can over-ride statute law in such circumstances. It is also a different case if an organization is no longer able to rely on any statutory permission to copy. It would be extremely difficult to prove that copying from a market research report was fair dealing in, for example, a company run for profit.

Many videos carry the statement 'licensed for home use only', or 'may not be performed in clubs, prisons or schools'. Unless the videos have been purchased under such conditions of sale, they may be ignored in an educational establishment as the playing of videos in these establishments is permitted so long as the audience is not public. See also Chapter 2, page 28.

Unlawful contractual restrictions

Under the database regulations, lawful users of a database are authorized to do anything necessary to enable them to access and use the contents whether under licence to use or not: any term or condition in any contract which accompanies the database which purports to prohibit or restrict this lawful use can be ignored. Similarly a contract may not restrict lawful users from extracting or reutilizing *insubstantial* parts of a database which has been made available to the public in any manner. See also Chapter 4, pages 51–2.

Copyright waivers

If a rights holder waives copyright on his/her works, it does not mean that there is no copyright in the works but that the rights holder has decided not to exploit the copyright and allows the material or data to be copied and used freely. However, 'used freely' may mean that the material may be used only within certain defined limits, e.g. copyright notices on some websites that state that copyright in the information on their site is waived for particular uses. The material is usually core (sometimes called raw) data because value has not been added. If value has been added, it usually indicates that the work is being exploited, e.g. published, and is therefore not covered by the waiver. The Crown copyright waiver (see below) is a good example where, for certain materials, copyright has been waived to ensure 'a light touch management'.

Crown copyright review

Following a Government review of Crown copyright in 1998 where the abolition of copyright for Crown works was debated, the Government issued a White Paper entitled *The Future Management of Crown Copyright* in 1999. Included were proposals to 'provide a blueprint for the future management of Crown copyright facilitating access to, and re-use of, official information'. In the White Paper the Government indicated that it was trying to achieve a balance between communicating information to its citizens and making a return on investment by trading that information. The Crown makes millions of pounds annually from tradable information, e.g. the mapping activities of Ordnance Survey, and there was an obvious reluctance to lose this income.

It was decided, therefore, that Crown copyright would not be abolished but that in the interests of a more transparent and open government, the copyright in certain categories of officially published material would be waived. The waiver (described below) does not extend to tradable information so any use, other than statutorily permitted, of the tradable revenue-generating material would have to be with permission or licence. Nor does the waiver apply to HMSO publications and publications printed by The Stationery Office.

The White Paper included guidance on policy making for those managing Crown copyright works. Subsequently, HMSO issued Guidance Notes to government departments, agencies and all users of Crown copyright protected material designed to alert, guide and advise on publishing and copyright issues. See Chapter 10, page 170 for details.

Crown copyright waiver

The copyright in all UK statutory material, i.e. Acts of Parliament and Statutory Instruments, is waived. Details covering primary and secondary legislation, including explanatory notes, in England, Wales and Northern Ireland are given in Guidance Note 6 at the HMSO website. For Scottish legislation, the Queen's Printer for Scotland has issued similar guidance (Guidance Note 1), also available at the HMSO website. See Chapter 10, page 170 for details. The legislation waiver also includes the typographical arrangement.

Reproductions must comply with the *waiver conditions*. These are:

- reproductions may only be made from the official version
- there must be no reproduction for the purposes of advertising or promoting a product or service or for promoting particular personal interests or views
- the material must not be used in a derogatory or misleading manner
- it must be reproduced accurately and acknowledged.

Provided that the waiver conditions are met, the following are permitted:

- reproducing and publishing the material in any medium
- making multiple copies for distribution or sale
- reproducing the material on free and subscription websites accessible via the internet
- reproducing the material on intranet sites
- making single or multiple copies by photocopying or any other means, for the purposes of research or private study (note, there is no restriction on copying for commercial purposes)
- the making of single or multiple copies by libraries for the supply of copies to readers under the library regulations

- copying by libraries for the purposes of supplementing or replenishing their stocks
- making copies for circulation throughout an organization whether in the public or private sector
- reproduction within the context of seminar or training packs
- reproduction within student theses or dissertations
- translations into other languages.

Other Crown copyright material subject to the waiver includes:

- government press notices
- government forms
- government consultative documents, e.g. Green Papers (even though they may be charged publications)
- government documents featured on official departmental websites (unless there is a clear statement to the contrary on the website)
- Headline Statistics, including high level statistics which are often published in the form of an ONS First Release (note that underlying statistical data may be subject to specific licensing arrangements)
- published papers of a scientific, technical or medical nature
- texts of ministerial speeches and articles (does not include constituency speeches)
- unpublished public records.

Parliamentary copyright waiver

The Crown copyright review dealt only with Crown material. Parliamentary material such as bills was not subject to the waiver although limited permission to copy bills and other Parliamentary copyright material was given in various HMSO 'Dear Librarian' letters. The latest version was issued in September 1996 and revised in March 2001 and is available at the HMSO website.

Bills and explanatory notes to bills of the UK Parliament are now covered by a Parliamentary copyright waiver which is explained in Guidance Note 14, available at the HMSO website. The waiver conditions are:

- reproduction must be made from the official version, i.e. the text ordered to be printed by either house and which bears a house printing number, or text downloaded from an official website: i.e. this would not cover copying from a text produced by a commercial law publisher
- the material must be reproduced or translated accurately and in a manner and context which is not misleading

- it must not be used in connection with advertising, endorsement or in any derogatory fashion, or in any circumstances which are knowingly libellous or slanderous
- when published, it must not be passed off as the official version: i.e. it must not bear any official symbols or insignia, e.g. the chained portcullis, and the ISBN must be removed
- care must be taken to identify the relevant stage of a bill when printing extracts
- reproductions must be acknowledged with an appropriate text.

Subject to the above conditions, the permitted uses under the waiver are:

- downloading and printing from official websites
- reproducing and publishing in any medium
- making multiple copies (including for sale)
- news reporting
- translating
- making available on the internet or an intranet
- hypertext linking to Parliament's website
- copying by users for research or private study, and by librarians for readers
- copying by prescribed libraries (ss. 41 and 42)
- student copying and use, e.g. in theses and dissertations.

More details are given in Guidance Note 14.

Apart from bills and explanatory notes, all other Parliamentary copyright material is still covered by the 'Dear Librarian' letter, i.e. it is not subject to the Parliamentary copyright waiver but copying greater than permitted under statute is allowed. There is also a similar 'Dear Publisher' letter. The materials still affected by this letter are: Lords and Commons Official Reports (Hansard), House business papers, including journals of both Houses, Lords minutes, the vote bundle, Commons order books, the Commons public bill lists and statutory instruments lists, the *Weekly Information Bulletin* and the *Sessional Information Digest*; other Parliamentary papers, including command papers and reports of select committees of both Houses.

The above may be copied within the following limitations:

- a single copy of an entire title or document for individual requesters is permitted except in educational establishments where each student may receive his/her own copy
- only one copy may be made to use within any organization
- no further distribution may be made to other individuals or organizations
- multiple copies of an extract or extracts of up to 30% of a whole work or one

complete chapter or equivalent, whichever is the greater, may also be made without permission or charge.

The 'Dear Librarian' letter also has conditions of copying: 'As you would expect, reproduction is NOT allowed in connection with advertising or endorsement, nor in any circumstances which, in the view of HMSO's Licensing Division, are potentially libellous or slanderous of individuals, companies or organizations. In addition its use must not give rise to unfair or misleading selection or undignified association.'

The Official Journal of the EU

A generous attitude is adopted towards copying from the Official Journal (OJ) as, similar to copying from Crown and Parliamentary material, it is in the EU's interest to disseminate the information contained therein. However, when photocopying it is advisable to stick to fair-dealing amounts (i.e. extracts limited to 5%, etc.) as the generous attitude does not extend to the typographical arrangement. There is no limitation to the number of items allowed to be copied from any individual issue of the OJ if they are re-keyed, but the inclusion of photocopies of OJ texts requires permission in writing from the Office for Official Publications of the European Communities. For those with a CLA licence, the OJ is covered by the CLA licence repertoire.

Web copyright notices

Many websites may be entered only after a contract has been agreed. This can either be negotiated beforehand, such as a subscription contract to an online journal where payment is required, or can be done on-screen by filling in details and agreeing terms. However, there are some content providers on the internet who may have waived copyright on their material altogether (e.g. material on Government departmental websites; see above), or waived it for personal or educational uses, so it makes sense to look at any copyright notices on websites to establish whether copying greater than permitted under copyright law is allowed. Many professional websites will have legal notices where a copyright statement will be included. An example of a copyright notice on a website where permission to copy for certain purposes is given in Figure 5.2.

Some notices on websites explicitly state that a copy may be downloaded to print or e-mailed to a friend. Implicit permission to copy may be given on others, but in these cases it would be foolish to assume that implicit permission extended to copying other than for private study or non-commercial research. In any case one could always ask the website owner for permission. But never

Copyright in all contributions to this website remains with [*the company, etc.*]. [*The company*] holds exclusive rights in respect of electronic publication and dissemination. No part of this website may be posted or in anyway mirrored on the world wide web or any other part of the internet without permission from [*the company*]. No link should be made to this site without permission from [*the company*].

Subject to this, permission is granted to download items for off-line reading and use subject to the following conditions:

- printouts are not sold for commercial purposes
- [*the company's*] name remains attached to any copies.

Permission is granted to download articles, store them electronically on disk, and make multiple copies for [*educational or personal*] purposes subject to the following condition:

no charge is made for access to users within the educational establishment.

Please contact [*the company*], if necessary, for clarification of these terms, or if you wish to use the material outside of the permissions given above.

Figure 5.2   An example of a web copyright notice

forget that if material is difficult to access and copy, e.g. it is accessed via a password, it is clear that content providers are not waiving their copyright, and so conditions of use should be respected. Similarly, reading conditions of access on-screen, and clicking to say that these are understood and accepted, means one has entered into a form of contract, and the terms should be respected. One should negotiate with content providers for uses over and above these terms.

Ten things to remember from this chapter

- if projected copying is not allowed under statute, one must obtain authorization directly from rights holders or their representatives
- permission to copy should preferably be given in writing
- never assume that if a rights holder does not respond to a request by a given time that consent has been given
- it is important to read and be aware of contractual terms and conditions
- it is important to be clear about what is wanted from a licence before negotiation
- terms and conditions are just as important as the costs of licensing
- avoid contracts which try to reduce copying or uses allowed under statute

- be aware of prohibitive statements
- legislative material may be copied freely, subject to non-burdensome waiver conditions
- be aware of web copyright notices.

6 Copyright compliance: licensing solutions

In this chapter you will learn about:

■ the importance of licensing
■ the various collecting societies
■ the different licensing schemes that are available.

In the previous chapter, guidance was given on what to expect from a contract or licence to copy and use copyright protected material. This chapter outlines the available sectoral and cross-sectoral licensing schemes for different materials, and describes some of the significant terms and conditions.

The importance of licensing

The 1988 Act explicitly encourages licensing for uses over and above statute. For example, in the educational exception, section 36 (1), it is stated that reprographic copies of passages from published works may be made by or on behalf of an educational establishment for the purposes of instruction, and then goes on to state, in section 36 (3), that this would not apply if there were licences available authorizing the copying and that the person making the copies knew or should be aware of that fact. Another example is in section 60, covering abstracts: if there is a certified licensing scheme available, then the exception to be able to copy abstracts accompanying scientific and technical journal articles freely is no longer applicable.

Since the 1988 Act, copyright licensing has grown in importance. The number of licensing agencies which have become established since 1989 has also grown. Information professionals, having been made increasingly aware of the limits of statutory copying and use, and the accompanying risks, have sought to reduce the liability of their organizations by seeking a licensing solution.

A licensing scheme, according to section 116 of the Act, is a scheme setting out:

(a) the classes of case in which the operator of the scheme, or the person on whose behalf he acts, is willing to grant copyright licences, and
(b) the terms on which licences would be granted in those classes of case; and for this purpose a 'scheme' includes anything in the nature of a scheme, whether described as a scheme or as a tariff or by any other name.

A licensing body is defined as 'a society or other organisation which has as its main object . . . the negotiation or granting, either as owner or prospective owner of copyright or as agent for him, of copyright licences, and whose objects include the granting of licences covering works of more than one author.'

Certified schemes

The Act also specifies that some licensing schemes have to be certified by the Secretary of State for Trade and Industry (s. 143). Educational off-air recording, public lending, the copying of abstracts and the provision of subtitled copies of broadcasts all require certification. The relevant schemes that have been certified are the Educational Recording Agency and the Open University off-air recording schemes. To date, there is no licensing scheme for abstracts.

There are many licensing schemes in the UK which are not required to be certified by the Secretary of State. For example, those run by the Copyright Licensing Agency and the Newspaper Licensing Agency are not accountable to the government. However, licensees of these schemes and any other licensing scheme have the opportunity to bring any licensing dispute to the Copyright Tribunal (see Chapter 7, page 126). These licensing bodies – sometimes called reproductive rights organizations (RROs), licensing agencies or collecting societies – have a monopoly over their licensing output, and so can, in theory (and sometimes in practice), impose terms without much or even any negotiation. Many users are demanding, therefore, that there should be some accountability. Although appealing to the Copyright Tribunal is an option, there is an obvious reluctance to bring in the Tribunal by all but the largest of consortia. There has been some discussion of a possible EC Directive in this area, but at the time of writing this appears to be on the back burner. In the meantime, the Patent Office is encouraging licensing bodies and user groups to agree a code of practice. The Libraries and Archives Copyright Alliance (see Chapter 10, page 164) is following this.

Benefits of having a licence

Having a licence should bring some peace of mind regarding liability (though arguably compliance can sometimes bring its own difficulties!). Licensed copying comes with an indemnity against accusations of copyright infringement provided all the terms and conditions are complied with. One of the other benefits of having a licence is that it does away with the need to complete the library regulations copyright declaration forms in prescribed libraries, although these would still be needed for supplying requests for unlicensed material or for individual requests.

The role of the licensing body

Licensing bodies normally have a mandate from their rights holders to operate on their behalf. This mandate allows the licensing body to grant licences, collect fees from licensees and to distribute these fees back to the rights holders.

Licensing bodies also have a duty to make the public aware of and respect copyright, as well as persuading institutions to take out licences. This can be a difficult role, as encouraging respect at the same time as using persuasive tactics can often cause conflict and confusion in users who may be unsure of whether taking out a licence is necessary. A licensing body will never admit it is not necessary.

Many licensing bodies have regular marketing campaigns. The CLA, for example, has an ongoing campaign called Copywatch, which relies on employees blowing the whistle on employers who condone copyright infringement. Licensing bodies have the power to institute legal proceedings in order to enforce the rights entrusted to them by their members. If a licensing body becomes aware of an organization involved in unauthorized photocopying or scanning, it will not hesitate to try to persuade that organization to buy a licence or, if there is resistance, instigate proceedings. This has become more of a threat since the change in the law regarding fair dealing. Most copying in an organization run for profit is now unlikely to fall under a statutory exception. This has increased the need for such organizations to obtain licences and has given more power to the licensing bodies to put pressure on them.

The licensing bodies whose schemes are described below are:

- the Copyright Licensing Agency, for copying from books and journals
- the Newspaper Licensing Agency, for copying from newspapers
- the Design and Artists Copyright Society, for copying of visual images
- the Educational Recording Agency and Open University Worldwide, for the recording off-air of terrestrial radio and television broadcasts for educational purposes
- HMSO, for UK government material
- Christian Copyright Licensing, for the copying of religious text and music
- Performing Right Society and Phonographic Performance Ltd, for the performance licensing of music and recorded music
- Video Performance Ltd, for the licensing of the performance of recorded films
- Mechanical Copyright Protection Society, for the copying (including downloading) of recorded music
- the British Standards Institution and the Ordnance Survey for the licensing of their material.

Several of these licensing bodies have formed themselves into a group called the Rights Industry Forum. Its remit is to review their various licensing schemes with a view to simplifying licences and improving conditions for users and to provide information on copyright compliance. More detailed information about the schemes described below is available on the websites of the individual bodies (see Appendix C, page 178). There is also a booklet available for schools, *A Guide to Licensing Copyright in Schools*, which covers all the relevant licensing schemes (for details see Chapter 10, page 170).

Book, journal and periodical licensing: The Copyright Licensing Agency

The Copyright Licensing Agency (CLA) is the main licensing body for reprographic copying from most UK books and periodicals, and those of an increasing number of other countries with which it has reciprocal agreements. The CLA is non-profit making and is jointly owned by the Authors' Licensing and Collecting Society (ALCS) and the Publishers Licensing Society (PLS). The CLA also has an Artistic Works Licence agreement with the Design and Artists Copyright Society (DACS) to allow photocopying of artistic works from published material in the CLA repertoire.

- ALCS collects fees on behalf of its members. In order to benefit from a possible payment, authors have to register themselves and their works. Works are identified by their ISBNs and ISSNs.
- PLS is similar to ALCS in that it collects monies on behalf of its publishers.
- DACS represents the interests of visual artists of all disciplines, including fine art and photography. It also deals with primary as well as secondary rights for some of its members.

All UK state schools, colleges of further education, universities and institutes of higher education, schools and colleges in the private sector, most government departments, the NHS, some industry sectors and many commercial companies are licensed by the Copyright Licensing Agency to make photocopies within clearly defined limits from books, journals and periodicals in their collections.

The CLA distributes monies collected from licensees to ALCS, PLS and DACS as compensation for the copying of their works. This is mainly based on a system of sampling surveys among licensed institutions. Organizations are selected to take part in such a survey for one year, which entails record keeping of all items copied. Surveys do not work, however, in the profit-making sector where there is a need for commercial confidentiality. In these cases, monies are distributed against holdings: e.g. if a company holds a copy of a work, it is assumed that a certain amount of copying takes place and the authors, publishers and artists, etc., are compensated accordingly.

The following section outlines the main terms and conditions which frequently appear in a basic CLA licence, and some details of the licences available to different sectors.

The licence

Licensees are granted permission to copy and distribute any material in territories covered by the licence as long as photocopies made are not on the list of excluded works or categories. Permission to copy is normally site-specific, i.e. allowed only on the licensed premises housing the licensed collection. So, for example, if an authorized person from a licensed educational establishment or company wished to make multiple copies of items from journals or published editions contained in a library elsewhere, then such copying would not be covered by their CLA basic licence.

The licence allows the distribution of copies by fax as long as there is no processing or manipulation of the material and no long-term storage involved. In other words, once the copy has been received, the electronic intermediate copy is deleted either by the machine or manually.

CLA standard limits on copying

Having a CLA licence does not mean that unrestricted copying is permitted. Authorized users are limited to making multiple copies of reasonable, one could say, insubstantial extracts. A typical photocopying licence allows the photocopying of no more than 5% of any item from the licensed collection; or one chapter not exceeding 30 pages in length; or one article from a journal issue not exceeding 30 pages in length; or the entire report of a case from a published report of judicial proceedings. Multiple amounts are negotiable: up to 9, 19 or 29 copies, or even more, depending on what is needed. Some organizations have negotiated to allow the copying of two articles from a single journal issue.

Coverage and excluded works and categories

The works in the CLA repertoire are not negotiable. Licensees have access to the whole repertoire whether they want it all or not. The CLA has reciprocal agreements with many other similar collecting societies in other countries. Currently the list includes: Australia, Canada (including Quebec), Denmark, France, Finland, Germany, Greece, Iceland, Ireland, the Netherlands, New Zealand, Norway, South Africa, Spain, Sweden, Switzerland and the United States (however, not all US publishers participate). In the near future it may expand to include Belgium, Mexico, Singapore and Hong Kong. Discussions have also taken place with Italy and Austria.

Although the CLA includes most books and journals, it has a large list of excluded categories and works which should always be checked before copying. The list may be examined on the CLA website. This does not always mean that works on the excluded list may not be copied. Some works may be covered by another licence, e.g. newspapers or OS maps. An excluded work or category may also mean that the copyright owner will allow copying to a greater extent than statute, e.g. copying permitted publications in schools and colleges, or the HMSO waiver material.

Normal obligations of the licensee

Licensees are obliged to make sure authorized persons are aware of the terms and conditions of the licence; to display CLA user guidelines adjacent to copying equipment; and to acknowledge the authors of works copied. Copies made may not be further exploited for financial gain although a nominal charge for copies may be made if applicable. Quite often in the CLA licences, it states that only original licensed material should be used to make copies. This means that the making of copies from photocopies made under a statutory provision, e.g. section 41, copying for stock, and section 42, copying to replace an original, is not permitted. However, some of the licences allow the making of a copy from a BL copyright-cleared copy, e.g. the HEI licence, so it is important to check.

Indemnity

Licensees, provided they do not breach the conditions of the licence, are indemnified against accusations of infringement when copying from the licensed material. The CLA will, therefore, cover any costs incurred should there be a case.

The CLARCS licence

The CLA Rapid Clearance System (CLARCS) is the telephone, fax, e-mail and internet based clearance service run by the CLA where, subject to the conditions of the licence and payment of fees, permissions are given to copy above the agreed standard limits of the basic licence. If there is a need to copy more than the basic licence allows, some licensees may take advantage of CLARCS. Notable exceptions to this are the further and higher education licences where CLARCS clearance is no longer an option. The CLA has indicated that it seems likely that the CLARCS licence will also disappear for all other sectors in due course.

CLA digitization licences

The CLA has introduced digital licensing to allow the scanning of print-on-paper materials for use on an organization's intranet. It does not extend to publicly available sites on the internet. So, for example, an educational establishment could offer access to distance learning students. For most licensees, the CLA licence to digitize for these purposes is still a transactional one, which means that every item required to be scanned has to be cleared. Also, only works for which the CLA has a positive mandate are offered, and fees are determined by rights holders themselves. Once cleared for digitization, a work may be accessed only by designated employees. The digitized works may be made available and may also be printed off, photocopied and distributed.

The CLA is now beginning to offer scanning (e-licensing) as well as photocopying in its basic licences. This comes with restrictions, including limited storage. See below under the core business licence (pages 95–6) for an example of the full details of terms and conditions. The public sector (central government departments, public bodies and public sector organizations) and the FE sector have also been given the digital option. The CLA has indicated that the other sectors will be given the opportunity to take advantage of this new scheme in their future licences if there is sufficient demand. The most likely time for this is when licences are up for renegotiation in the renewal process.

The requirement to store scanned material, other than for statutory archive purposes, is urgent, and many organizations are asking the CLA to allow this. It is likely that this will be offered as an enhancement in future licences. However, as most rights holders are very worried about the potential for copyright infringement of their material, such a licence is likely to be tightly controlled and expensive.

CLA sectoral licensing

The following section contains some details about various current sectoral CLA licensing schemes in order to illustrate which sectors have specific licences and to highlight the differences between them. It makes sense also to check the relevant institution's licence, as subtle changes may have taken place during the renewal process since this was written (October 2003). The CLA website also has information on all its current schemes, including user guidelines. Although the main sector schemes are outlined below, the list is by no means comprehensive. For example, many of the industry sectors have their own variations on the business licence, but apart from the model licence for law firms, details of these have not been included. This is mainly because the changes to the core business licence will mean that many of the industry sector licences will follow suit and incorporate scanning upon renewal.

Licences for publicly funded bodies

Government

The CLA has licensed many government departments and agencies. A typical government departmental licence allows the copying of up to nine copies of one chapter or 5% of a book, two articles from a periodical, and the whole report of one case from law reports. Up to 19 copies may be made for designated committees. Copies may be supplied to colleagues within and without the department. Items may also be scanned and sent via e-mail. The new public sector licence also allows copying of any number of articles from a journal if the issue of the journal is dedicated to a particular theme. Licence fees are based on the number of professional employees likely to undertake photocopying from licensed material. What is a 'professional employee' is negotiable.

Local authorities

Many local authorities are also licensed by the CLA. However, this does *not* cover copying in public libraries. Authorized persons (those who may make and distribute or those who are permitted to receive copies) are directors, officers or employees or anyone with an existing contractual relationship with the local authority, or anyone with an interest in the material copied as a consequence of a legal, statutory or equitable obligation. The licence fee is calculated on the number of professional employees – those employees on or above spinal column point (SCP) 39 or equivalent.

The standard limits on copying apply, except that authorized persons are permitted to copy or receive two items from any single issue of a journal or periodical. Also, if an issue of a journal is on a particular theme, any number of articles may be taken from the issue dealing with the theme. Up to 9 copies may be made for any purpose and up to 19 copies may be made for designated committees. Designated committees are defined as committees which have an advisory, executive, tribunal or consultative function. Ad hoc committees would not therefore be covered by this definition. Items may also be scanned and sent by e-mail. Any copies needed above these amounts need clearance, so a CLARCS licence must be obtained. However, licensees have to pay for all copies not just the extra ones needed. For example, if ten copies were required, all ten would have to be paid for, not just the extras. Similarly, if a committee wanted to make and distribute 25 copies, all 25 would have to be paid for.

The NHS

The CLA agreed a landmark licence with NHS England in 2002. NHS

Northern Ireland is also licensed. A similar scheme for NHS Scotland had already been negotiated in 2000. At the time of writing, discussions were still taking place with NHS Wales. Details of the licence for NHS England is described below.

Subject to the conditions of the licence, the licence allows authorized persons to make or permit the making of photocopies from the licensed material on the premises occupied by the licensee and to distribute such copies by or to authorized persons. An 'authorized person' is 'any director, officer, or employee of the licensee or lay representative or any other person having as a consequence of an existing contractual relationship with the licensee or as a consequence of a statutory, legal or equitable obligation of the licensee an interest in material which is the subject of the copies'. In other words, employees of the licensee (including those working under contract, temporary or otherwise) plus those who are connected to the licensee by a statutory, legal or equitable obligation, e.g. patients and walk-in users.

The NHS bodies covered by the licence include all NHS trusts, including ambulance trusts, primary care trusts and subsidiary bodies within trusts, e.g. patient liaison services and members of trust boards, and NHS health authorities, including special health authorities, e.g. the NHS Information Authority, NHS Direct and NHS Direct Online. Also licensed are general practitioners, including primary care groups. All other health organizations funded by the NHS are also covered.

The licence allows the making by authorized persons, on the licensed premises, of up to 15 photocopied extracts from licensed material for any particular purpose. The standard limits apply, except that two articles from a single issue of a journal or periodical may be copied, and any number of articles dealing with a particular theme within an issue of a journal may be copied. For designated committees it is permitted to make up to 25 copies for any single meeting. The definition of designated committee is 'any body or persons established by the Licensee having an advisory, consultative, tribunal or executive function'. An example of a designated committee could be a board or any established internal committee. It would not cover any ad hoc meeting of staff. Copying for this purpose would be limited to 15 copies.

For copying outside the terms of the licence, clearance is available from CLARCS (but see above: this is being phased out). The licensed institution would be charged for the total number of copies made rather than the extra copies. So if 17 copies were required for a particular purpose, the institution would be charged for all 17 not the two extras; or if there were 26 members at an internal meeting, all 26 copies would have to be paid for, not just the one extra.

Calculation of fees is based on the number of professional employees. Professional employees are defined as staff of higher executive office (HEO) grade or above or equivalent, and unrestricted principals or equivalent (UPEs) who are contracted to provide a service to the NHS.

The business licences

CLA core business licence

The revised terms for this licence were issued in 2002. This is the first of the new CLA licences which include scanning, so it is described in more detail. Subject to payment and the terms and conditions described below, the licence allows authorized persons to:

- make or permit the making of copies
- distribute or permit the distribution of copies to authorized persons
- scan material licensed for scanning to produce digital copies
- make digital copies available, or permit the making available, within the UK, in both cases solely within the licensee's intranet (this includes e-mailing)
- make copies of copies.

Scanning and distribution of copies is limited to the UK only.
   The conditions for copying, distribution and scanning are that:

- the licensee must own an original or a copyright-fee-paid copy of the material
- copying and scanning are restricted to the standard limit on amounts (see above)
- copying is for any single occasion or purpose
- copies may not be sold or disposed of for gain
- copies may not be rented or loaned outside the company
- copies are for the internal information purposes of the organization (this includes the training of authorized persons as long as no payment or remuneration is received in the training process)
- copies must not be used for marketing or promotional purposes
- copies made should not substitute directly or indirectly for the purchase of the original: e.g. if a work is available for sale or hire then it should be purchased or hired rather than copied
- black and white (or halftone) copies may be made of works in colour provided that no colour separations are made.

There are further restrictions on making digital copies. Licensees are prohibited from:

- editing, amending, manipulating, adding to or deleting from digital copies or authorizing anyone else to do the same
- digitally manipulating copies (apart from those needed by a person with a visual impairment)
- making copies available on a publicly accessible website or linking digitized copies to external or third-party websites
- making copies for publication, repackaging, distribution or any dissemination including communication to the public or making available except as permitted by the licence
- storing digital copies on a server or systematically indexing them with the intention of creating an electronic library. Copies may, however, be stored as part of the back-up or archival process or where there is a legal requirement. They may also be stored indefinitely on the C:\ drive of a computer but may not be kept on a central shared database.

Licensees are obliged to:

- delete offending material from wherever it is stored if the copyright holder thinks that the digitized material has infringed copyright or is of a defamatory nature, obscene or otherwise unlawful
- acknowledge the author of a digitized artistic work if the name of the author/artist is adjacent to the work to be scanned.

The cost of the core business licence is calculated on the type of business sector and the number of 'professional employees'. This covers personnel whose work involves literature use relevant to the industrial sector concerned. The number of professional employees and the copying amounts are negotiable. There are three bands of charges which are determined according to the main business activity of the organization, as defined by the standard industrial classification (SIC) code. The three bands of charges per professional employee per annum are currently: Band A, £27.87; Band B, £18.58; and Band C, £9.29. These prices are exclusive of VAT. For example, large industries such as those in the food and energy industries would pay Band A fees, whereas those in the general manufacturing sector would be in Band B. Charges for CLARCS are on top of the basic tariff and are levied at a cost per page or per article basis.

The CLA small business licence

The Copyright Licensing Agency has introduced a simplified licence to copy (e-mail, fax or scan) book, journal and magazine extracts for businesses with up to 50 employees. The licence removes the need to classify employees into professional and non-professional. The fee structure at the time of writing is that businesses employing up to 10 people will be charged a flat fee of £95 per year, and those employing between 11 and 50 employees will be charged £295.

Law Society model licence for law firms

The latest licence was concluded in 2001 and was due to expire in August 2003 but has been extended pending renegotiation. The standard limits on copying apply. Licensees may opt for making up to either 9 or 29 copies. If required, there is an option for circulating internal press cuttings, and there is a special CLARCS rate for circulating contents pages.

Press cuttings agencies licence

The United Kingdom Media Monitoring Association (UKMMA) agreed a licence in May 2003 with the CLA to allow press cuttings agencies to deliver journal and magazine cuttings digitally to their clients. UKMMA is the trade body representing most of the UK's cuttings agencies. The agreement, which complements the business licence, allows agencies to scan paper publications and use OCR technology to find keywords and create cuttings. These can then be distributed to clients by a password-protected dedicated web service and e-mail, as well as by fax and hard copy.

Enhanced business licence

The CLA has been in discussion regarding an enhanced business licence which would allow systematic storage of scanned material. Some industry sectors would like to do this. The pharmaceutical industry, for example, wants to be able to store all items about a specific product together. The CLA is in discussion with its members to give them a mandate to allow this.

The education licences

Schools

All schools in the UK are licensed by the CLA. The current licence, which expires in March 2004, covers all staff and pupils of the school. Whereas in previous licences there were separate licences for state and independent schools and regional differences, the schools licence is now the same for all UK schools. The only difference between them is in how they are administered and paid for. The CLA negotiates with LEAs for the administration of licences for schools in the state sector, and with the Independent Association of Preparatory Schools

(IAPS) for the administration of licences in the private sector. Schools licences in those LEAs which have opted out of state funding are handled by IAPS.

Extracts copied may not exceed 5% of a published volume or journal issue or, if greater, one chapter of a published edition (not exceeding 30 pages), one article not exceeding 30 pages from a journal or periodical, and no more than 10 pages from a short story or poem. Copying must not exceed that needed for one course of study or module. For example, each pupil in a class may have a copy, plus one for the teacher. In addition, copies may also be made for meetings of parents or governors.

The licence includes the copying of artistic works, and so graphic works (photographs, illustrations and diagrams, etc.) contained in licensed publications may be photocopied either on their own or as part of the extract. Schools are allowed to make enlarged copies and copies onto OHP acetates up to the above limits for the purposes of the National Literacy Strategy. This used to be an additional protocol which had to be paid for, but is now included in the licence.

Permission is given to make enlarged or reduced-size copies from items in the licensed collection (i.e. bought by the school and available to other pupils) for partially sighted pupils or staff for the purposes of instruction only, subject to certain conditions. Copies may not be made if there is a commercially available large-print version of the work. The limits of copying (up to 5% of a work, etc.) do not apply to large-print versions as long as the licensee ensures that the number of copies made does not exceed the number of partially sighted pupils or staff. Copies may not be edited or bound up with other copyright material, published or sold.

Although not a condition of the licence, the CLA recommends as good practice that extracts selected for photocopying should include bibliographic details.

Further education

This licence covers state-funded further education colleges, sixth forms and independent and vocational FE institutions in the UK. The current licence was renewed in 2003.

Students and staff are authorized to make and receive copies. The licence explicitly states that students include distant learners. The standard limitations on copying apply; i.e. no more than 5% of extracts from a published volume or issue of a journal, or, if greater, one complete chapter, or one article, or up to ten pages from a short story or poem contained in an anthology. Copying must not exceed that needed for one course of study or module. For example, each student in a class may have a copy, plus one for the tutor. Copies may also be made for meetings of staff managers or parents. Artistic works, i.e. photographs, illustrations and diagrams, contained in licensed publications may be photocopied. Copies of any extracts may also be made onto OHP acetates but artistic works may not be made into slides. (See DACS Slide Collection Licensing Scheme below.)

If more copies than permitted are required then licensed institutions have to apply for permission from rights holders, as application to CLARCS is no longer an option for further or higher education.

The course pack restriction under the previous licence has now been removed and so copying for producing a course or study pack is covered by the licence. Any copies sold to students must not make a profit.

Fees are calculated annually based on the number of full-time equivalent students (FTEs) multiplied by a fixed fee.

Permission is given to make enlarged or reduced-size copies from items in the licensed collection (i.e. bought by the licensee and available to other students) for partially sighted students or staff for the purposes of instruction only, subject to certain conditions. Copies may not be made if there is a commercially available large-print version of the work. The limits of copying (up to 5% of a work, etc.) do not apply to large-print versions as long as the licensee ensures that the number of copies made does not exceed the number of partially sighted students or staff. Copies may not be edited or bound up with other copyright material, published or sold. This indicates that such copies may not be included in bound course packs but could be included in a loose-leaf version. Copies made under this provision must not be put into a short loan collection.

Although not a condition of the licence, the CLA recommends as good practice that extracts selected for photocopying should include bibliographic details.

The CLA has been consulting this sector for some time concerning a pilot scheme for digitization of text (e-licensing). This licence is now available; it is in addition to the normal photocopying licence and so costs extra. It is remarkable for being the first blanket e-licence for education. Subject to terms and conditions, the licence allows:

- scanning extracts from licensed material
- storage of such copies on a networked server, i.e. the college intranet, a virtual learning environment (VLE) or a managed learning environment (MLE)
- storage of such copies on to individual PCs
- retyping extracts onto a word-processing package on a computer
- incorporating digital copies into presentation packages, e.g. PowerPoint™
- sending copies by fax; and sending copies by e-mail to authorized users.

Copies made under the e-licence may be shared with similar licensed colleges.

Higher education

The previous HE institutions licence was referred to the Copyright Tribunal in

July 2000 by Universities UK (formerly the CVCP) and the CLA on the grounds that it was unreasonable. See Chapter 7, pages 131–2 for details. The latest licence, effective from August 2001, is not due for renewal until July 2006. It is likely therefore that the HE sector will be last in line to obtain the scanning licence or any other improvements until then. This licence applies to UUK and SCOP HE institutions. It is understood, also, that if an independent HEI was covered by the previous HE licence then this post Copyright Tribunal HE licence is also applicable to it.

Authorized persons are all recipients of instruction and staff of the HE institution. 'Recipients of instruction' means all students who attend courses of instruction included in the UCAS brochure of their HEI. Although it is not stated explicitly, it is understood that distance learning students are also included in this definition as long as they are on a course described in the UCAS brochure. There is in any case an obligation for the HEI to notify the CLA of the number of students taking part in courses away from the licensed premises. However, any courses of instruction which are not described in the UCAS brochure, e.g. short fee-paying courses, are *not* covered by the licence. Any copying for such courses has to be cleared with rights holders.

The licence allows multiple copying of items from the licensed collection limited to the number of students on a course of study, plus one for the lecturer. The standard limitations on copying apply: extracts of no more than 5% or one chapter from a published volume; or no more than one article from an issue of a serial publication or a set of conference proceedings; or up to ten pages from a short story or poem contained in an anthology; or the entire report of a single case in a set of published judicial proceedings. Any copying which is in excess of what is permitted under the licence has to be cleared with rights holders individually. Since the Copyright Tribunal decision, CLARCS licences are no longer an option for the higher education sector.

A copy of a photocopy may also be made, provided that either the HEI owns the original work or the copy has been obtained from a copyright-fee-paid service such as the BLDSC, in which case such copies must contain the document supply cover sheets. Also, if written permission has been obtained from a rights holder to copy a copy, the document granting the permission must be retained for inspection if required. No other copying of photocopies is permitted, so, for example, further copying of copies made under sections 41 or 42 (copying for stock or replacement by librarians) is not allowed under the licence.

Permission is given to make enlarged or reduced-size copies from items in the licensed collection (i.e. bought by the licensee and available to other students) for partially sighted students or staff for the purposes of instruction only, subject to certain conditions. Copies may not be made if there is a commercially available large-print version of the work. The limits of copying (up to 5% of a work, etc.) do not apply to large-print versions as long as the HEI ensures that the number of copies made does not exceed the number of partially sighted students or staff. Copies may not be edited or bound up with other copyright material, published or sold. This indicates that such copies may not be included in bound course packs but could be included in a loose-leaf version. Copies made under this provision must not be put into a short loan collection.

The licence includes the copying of artistic works, and so graphic works (photographs, illustrations and diagrams, etc.) contained in licensed publications may be photocopied either on their own or as part of the extract.

The course pack restriction contained in the previous licence has been removed. Course packs may, therefore, be compiled (within the copying limitations of course) and given to students. Students can be charged for the copies as long as this is for cost-recovery only. No profit must be made.

The licence does not contain a definition of a short loan collection, and the only mention of a short loan collection is in relation to copying for partially sighted students and staff. Therefore, it is understood that the restrictions which applied in the previous licence have been removed. This means that course packs may now be kept in short loan, provided any copies which may potentially be made by students do not exceed the number of students on one course of study, etc. Copies of copies may also be included in short loan provided they comply with the conditions described above. Cover sheets are required if the copies have been obtained from a document supply service, but do not appear to be required if copies are made from the HEI's own collection. It would not be advisable to put fair-dealing copies made by lecturers or copies obtained under sections 41–42 (copying for stock or replacement by librarians) in short loan if they are likely to be on-copied systematically by students.

The CLA HEI licence, like all licences, is a solution to the problem of systematic single copying and multiple copying. The licence is also without prejudice to any copying which is allowed under statute, e.g. fair dealing and copying by librarians. However, the restriction on research for a commercial purpose introduced by the Copyright Directive implementation does not, unfortunately, appear to be covered by a CLA blanket licence, at least not in HE. It is understood that this licence covers only multiple copying (including systematic single copying) and not copies made by individuals under fair dealing. So, any individual copying for research (or even private study) which is judged to be commercial (see Chapter 2, pages 18–19) has to be authorized in some other way. This concerns some HE institutions that allow the public to use the photocopier, as there may be some copying on these machines that is likely to fall under this restriction. Regular meetings take place between the CLA and UUK and SCOP, and this has been one of the topics under discussion. In the meantime, the CLA may have resolved such copying by having a walk-in user scheme using stickers (see below).

Annual fees are calculated on the number of FTEs multiplied by the current fee. The number of students has to be declared annually. The fee increases annually in line with the retail price index. FTEs are full-time students plus part-time students expressed as full-time students. For example: two part-time students would equal one full-time student, so 10 full-time students plus 20 part-time students would equal 20 FTEs. However, distance learning students have to be classed as full-time students even though they may not all study full time.

The scheme only covers those works for which the CLA has a mandate, so it will not resolve the problem of how to authorize copying for a commercial purpose from works not covered. Permission will still have to be sought from rights holders unless the CLA offers an indemnity for such works.

Licensing scheme for visually impaired persons

At the time of writing (October 2003) this scheme is still being finalized. Certain approved organizations representing visually impaired people, e.g. the RNIB, will be eligible to apply for a VIP licence to allow the making of multiple accessible copies of works in any format for use by visually impaired persons. The licence conditions follow the restrictions on making multiple copies under the Copyright (Visually Impaired Persons) Act 2002 which amended the Copyright, Designs and Patents Act 1988 (s. 31B) (Chapter 2, page 33).

Transactional licences

Walk-in user scheme

The CLA, representatives of libraries including the BL, and rights holder representatives held extensive discussions in 2003 to resolve the problem of copying from books and journals by those users who are no longer authorized under statute to copy under fair dealing (s. 29), i.e. copying for a commercial purpose. These are users of publicly accessible libraries, such as public libraries, the BL Reading Room and other libraries, including some academic institutions, which allow access to the public. The solution suggested is for a sticker (or voucher) scheme.

All prescribed not-for-profit libraries will be able to apply for books of stickers. These will be issued in books of 20 and will be supplied free of charge. Other libraries, which are not prescribed, will have to buy them. The stickers will be used in conjunction with numbered forms which will be supplied as a pad of 20 forms. The cost to the user of one sticker will be £9.00 (including VAT). Users wishing to make a copy will be given a form to complete which should describe the bibliographical details of the item to be copied. The user will then present the completed form and the £9.00 fee to the librarian, who will issue them with a peel-off sticker to be affixed to the photocopy. The top copy will be returned to the user as a receipt and the bottom copy will be retained by the library and then sent to the CLA with the copying fees.

Document delivery (supply) licences

Document supply is not included in the CLA basic licence so has to be dealt with separately. A document supply licence is applicable to any institution wanting to offer such a service. The licence allows the making of copies from licensed material and the subsequent distribution of such copies to clients. It therefore offers a solution to those prescribed libraries which are now unable to supply items for research needed for a commercial purpose because of the change in the law, as well as to organizations wishing to run a commercial document supply service. Distribution can be by post or by secure electronic delivery service, such as fax or Ariel.

In 2003 the British Library Document Supply Centre (BLDSC) revised its licensing agreement with the CLA to provide a copyright-fee-paid document delivery service. Other document delivery licences are being based on the BL scheme.

Document delivery licences are post-hoc transactional, which means that licensees are charged for the exact usage and are obliged to report to the CLA on what has been copied on a quarterly basis. Rights holders normally set the fees. There is a default fee for others.

Before negotiating a document delivery licence, the CLA needs to have an idea of the variety of titles that are being copied in order to work out the likely charges for each title, and which items are on the excluded works list. With these licences, there may be more excluded works than in the blanket licence, as publishers have to opt in. The CLA also has to have an idea of the volume of copying.

Copying is unlimited. The licence also allows the copying of contents pages of a year's issue of any periodical publication, which means that licensees may offer a current awareness service based on this.

Licensed copies may be distributed electronically. If copies are sent this way, then the electronic copy must be deleted once a paper copy has been taken. No storage for later use is allowed. Also, copies sent electronically must include a standard statement to the effect that the work has been supplied by the (named) licensee; that no further copying of the paper copy may be made unless authorized; and that the electronic copy may not be stored or retransmitted or used again. Copies sent in paper form must also bear a standard statement forbidding any additional unauthorized copying.

Low-volume document delivery blanket licence

Discussions took place between CLA representatives and the learned societies in early 2003 on a licence to allow copying for commercial research purposes either under fair dealing or the library regulations following the Copyright Directive implementation. Although the transactional licence was an option, many of these institutions were not copying enough to warrant the additional administration. A low-volume blanket licence was therefore requested and agreed. These licences are being piloted for one year. Low volume means making 100 or fewer copies per month.

Newspaper Licensing Agency licensing schemes

The NLA is authorized by the publishers of certain newspapers to grant non-exclusive licences for the copying and distribution of newspaper cuttings. The NLA targets organizations in the commercial, education and non-profit sectors to take out licences to cover them for ad hoc copying and systematic copying. It has a reputation for hard-line persuasive tactics in ensuring compliance. One notable case was *NLA v. Marks and Spencer* (see Chapter 7, pages 130–1). The NLA repertoire consists of all the UK national newspapers, most major UK regional newspapers and some major foreign titles.

Types of licence and the fee tariff

There is a standard licence which covers the copying requirements of most organizations, and there are licences covering the copying in educational establishments, schools, charities and professional partnerships.

The fee tariff can look quite complicated. It is linked to the different copying requirements of licensees. Organizations may require a basic standard licence covering ad hoc copying, or a basic licence plus a licence to copy one or two titles (for supplying to clients of public relations consultancies and trade or professional associations), or a basic licence plus a licence to copy systematically, i.e. on a regular basis for internal management or educational purposes. There are also additional charges for scanning and digital distribution. For copying from non-national UK (i.e. regional) weekly newspapers there is a supplemental fee of 0.5% of the basic charge. Sunday newspapers and foreign titles are charged at 1% of the basic charge.

There is also a requirement to pay an indemnity fee for copying in the preceding years if this is applicable. If licensees can provide evidence that there has been a policy in place to discourage copying of newspapers then this will not apply. Obviously, any statutory copying under the exceptions should not be part of this equation as these are permitted acts, but if potentially infringing copies have been made over the preceding years the NLA provides an indemnity to cover for any legal action taken. Discounts on the fee paid for past years' copying are available if a prompt response to take out a licence is made to the NLA. Details of the fee structure are available on the NLA website.

The prices quoted below were correct as from 1 January 2004.

The basic annual fee covers the ad hoc copying of newspapers in the NLA repertoire. Ad hoc means simply copying on an *occasional* basis, so, for example, if someone in an organization spots an article in a newspaper which is relevant to the organization, the organization may make copies of the article and distribute them to whoever needs a copy. This is not the same as copying on a regular basis. Such copying would be seen as systematic and is extra to the basic licence.

The basic fee is calculated on the total number of personnel (the more there are, the more you pay) or, if the licensee is a commercial company, on the total turnover in the preceding financial year, whichever produces the lower fee. For example, a company with 50 staff would pay £170 (based on current rates) even if its turnover was over £100m. Equally, if a company's turnover was between £100m and £250m but it had over 10,000 employees, the fee would be £1595.

The systematic copying fee is based on an audit of copies made in the whole organization taken over a period of not more than four weeks. From this an annual figure is projected which is multiplied by the number of staff copying and the cost per copy. (For educational establishments it is the number of FTEs plus staff.) At the time of writing this is 2.7p for all UK titles and 5.3p for foreign titles. For example: if, during a two-week period, 30 copies were made from UK newspapers by two employees, the calculation for a year would be 30 (copies) x 26 (two weeks) x 2 (people) x 2.7p = £421–20.

There is a separate additional tariff for public relations consultancies and trade and professional associations, and costs depend on how many cuttings are made, whether they are from national, regional or foreign newspapers, and whether they are photocopied or faxed to clients or sent by e-mail. For example, the fee for an organization that makes up to 3 photocopy/faxes of any one cutting from national newspapers is £48. The fee for up to 45 e-mailed copies is £108.

For digital copying, there are two options available and both depend on an initial audit being taken. Option 1 is based on the number of copies taken in a year. If, for example, an organization makes anything up to 75,000 digital copies a year, the price per copy is £0.45 with a minimum payment of £300. Above 75,000 copies, the price per copy becomes cheaper. The second option, Option 2, is based on the number of staff and only ten cuttings per newspaper per day are allowed, although more may be negotiated. There is a minimum charge of £2500. If an organization chooses this option, the cost per year would be £2500 for up to 10 employees, £4170 for 10–25 employees, and so on, with the unit price reducing with the increase in staff.

The indemnity fee for the unlicensed years is a multiple of the first year fee to a maximum of six years, reflecting the statute of limitations, but these fees may be discounted. If an organization agrees to take out a licence within 8 weeks of being contacted by the NLA, there is a reduction of 2.5 years: within 12 weeks, the reduction is 1.5 years.

The licence

Depending on the type of organization and which fee structure an organization buys into, an NLA licence allows the making of photocopies of cuttings taken from the NLA repertoire. Copies may be distributed to clients, including by fax or e-mail.

NLA indemnifies a licensee, including any subsidiary or associated companies (within the UK only) against accusations of infringement for normal licensed copying and past copying (if applicable) and agrees to pay damages in any dispute.

Copying may only take place on the licensed premises. This is normally in the UK only. However, if a company is a subsidiary of a foreign parent company or has its own subsidiary or associated companies in another country, it may distribute copies to them provided this has been declared. The costs will obviously escalate to take account of the extra personnel worldwide.

If copying ad hoc, no more than 250 copies may be made of any one cutting taken from any one issue of a newspaper. Copies can be for internal management purposes or, if in education, for educational or instruction purposes, e.g. inclusion in study packs. The NLA must be approached to give written consent if more copies need to be made.

The licences excludes copying any artistic works (photographs, illustrations or advertisements) appearing in newspapers.

The digital copying fee allows an organization to scan and e-mail cuttings or to receive such copies digitally for internal e-mail distribution. Copies marked with 'ND' in the NLA repertoire may not be digitized. Copies made may not be stored for longer than seven days, after which time they must be permanently deleted from the system. Also, digital copies received from licensed press cuttings agencies, public relations consultancies or trade and professional organizations must be deleted after seven days. However, as the NLA requires that details of such copies must be kept for auditing purposes, it is allowed to keep downloaded print copies. In addition, trade or professional associations and PR consultancies must keep a record of recipient clients including contact details. This is to ensure that such clients are also licensed to distribute such copies internally. Obviously, with data protection in mind, consent has to be obtained from clients first.

Licence conditions

There is an obligation on licensees to inform all staff, including that of subsidiary and associated companies, of the limits of the licence, and to display NLA user guidelines, if available, by copying machines. At the present time, there are no NLA user guidelines.

Records of copies made must be kept and, if the NLA requests it, a copy of each cutting made as part of the auditing obligations must be sent to them. This is to ensure that royalties are distributed appropriately to rights holders.

Each copy or collation of copies must include the notice: 'NLA licensed copy. No further copies may be made except under licence.'

If requested, licensees are obliged to provide, within 30 days after the request, a certificate signed by a mutually approved professional to the effect that the licensee has complied with the terms of the licence.

The licence lasts for 12 months from commencement but may be renewed annually, subject to the licensee paying the requisite fee within 35 days after expiry. If an organization fails to pay within this time, this is a 'material breach of the licence'.

Special dispensations for charities and schools

Following an agreement between the NLA and the National Council for Voluntary Organisations (NCVO), many voluntary organizations can now benefit from a substantial reduction in fees or possibly pay nothing at all. The agreement means that all charities with a turnover less than £250,000, or fewer than five members of staff, will pay nothing for ad hoc copying. The licence fee would have been £92. Those registered charities which have more than five staff or a turnover of more than £250,000 qualify for a discount of £92 off their basic licence fee for ad hoc copying. Systematic and digital copying is additional but may also be subject to a discount. Application has to be made on the NLA website to qualify. Charities applying for a licence prior to July 2004 also qualified for a discount on the indemnity fee (if applicable) of 75%. If a charity wishes to copy systematically or digitally, a fee would obviously have to be paid. A registered charity or member of the Charities Institute in Scotland may apply for a licence to allow copying under the basic licence conditions. The NLA definition of a charity excludes any further or higher education establishment or 'organization whose primary purpose is other than the management of a charitable fund for which it has registered'.

Schools with pupils up to 16 years old are also entitled to apply for a free licence on condition that the application is completed online from the NLA website. The licence allows the making of copies under the basic ad hoc licence.

British Standards Institution licence

This is a licence for educational institutions that allows copying for class purposes. Special bulk discounts are available when whole documents are needed. Otherwise the licence permits copying of substantial portions of standard specifications, short of whole documents. Details are available from the British Standards Institution (see Appendix C, page 178).

Visual image licensing

Copying artistic works contained in books and journals is now covered by the CLA agreement with DACS so all their licences permit such copying. See under CLA above.

DACS

The Design and Artists Copyright Society, formed in 1983, is the collecting society which represents visual artists – artists and photographers – in the UK. It has reciprocal arrangements with other similar visual artists' collecting societies in Europe and the rest of the world. Like the CLA and NLA, it issues licences on behalf of its members, and collects and distributes monies owed to visual artists for uses of their copyright works. Some examples of uses of artistic works are on television, posters, leaflets, sleeves of sound and video recordings, websites, postcards, greetings cards and even on T-shirts. DACS's main way of recompensing artists for their works having been copied is different from how authors and publishers are recompensed because artistic works do not normally have any standard identifier. DACS, therefore, as part of its Payback service, encourages its members to write in if copies of their works have been seen on television or published in journals, etc.

Slide collection licensing scheme

The scheme which is most relevant to information professionals is the slide collection licensing scheme for higher and further education establishments which was developed with the guidance of a steering group of user representatives. This in itself was innovative and encouraging. Other licensing schemes have normally been devised without much, or even any, user input. DACS developed the scheme to enable educational establishments to reproduce images from books and journals onto slides for use as an educational resource.

The scheme is in two parts: an agreement to declare and pay for any existing collection; and an annual licence for making new slides. Organizations with an existing collection, including any illegally produced slides, are required to declare the approximate number in the collection and make a one-off payment. This payment is calculated according to the size of the collection. In return for payment and compliance with the terms of the agreement, DACS indemnifies the institution against claims of copyright infringement by artists for their works held in collections.

The annual licence permits establishments to produce new and add existing slides to the collection. A flat-rate fee is payable for the first year, and subsequent annual payments are calculated according to the number of slides added to the collection during each year.

The licensing scheme for slide collections permits the reproduction of up to ten copies for educational purposes of artistic works contained in published works onto slides, acetates or transparencies, and these may be stored in the library. Included in the definition of artistic works are: paintings, sculptures, collages, engravings or prints, drawings, photographs, other graphic works and works of artistic craftsmanship. It does not cover film stills, advertisements, mapping or trademarks.

The steering group is still active and the problems of the scheme are discussed regularly and eventually resolved. Some of the issues discussed have been the problems of communication, data returns and unnecessary detail. Another issue, which has still not been resolved satisfactorily, is what to do with personal collections of slides owned by individual lecturers. At present these do not come under the scheme as they are not housed in the library or even catalogued. These are arguably illegal collections and should be declared, paid for and legitimized. However, if they were to be declared, returns would still have to be made, as well as payments, and the question arises as to where the responsibility for this rests: with the individual lecturers who are unwilling to participate in or share the administration, let alone the sharing of their personal collections, or with the librarians, also unwilling to add to their present burden of licence administration and to pay for a collection which is not available to all.

Future schemes for digitization of visual images

Slide collections are not as popular as they once were, and DACS has noticed a downturn in the number of slides being made. The higher education sector has long been requesting to be allowed to digitize artistic works, rather than just put them onto slides, and to keep stored images in a networked internal collection for educational use. DACS has been consulting its members to see whether a suitable scheme can be worked out. The fear of piracy is still behind the reluctance by visual artists to permit digitization on a regular basis even with contractual restrictions, so obtaining a mandate may take time. There may be another solution if the participation by DACS in the CLA digitization initiatives continues. The test will be whether the storing of any scanned images is allowed for shared use.

Ordnance Survey

Ordnance Survey is the national mapping agency of Great Britain. Although its products are Crown copyright they are not covered by the Crown copyright waiver as described in Chapter 5, pages 80–1. OS produces revenue for the government, and as such is a designated tradable information body.

Details of all the licences on offer from OS are available on its website. A few details of the more relevant ones are given below. OS also publishes various product information leaflets on the website, as well as frequently asked questions.

Pan-government agreement

OS has concluded a pilot agreement with central government to enable many government departments and agencies to have access to Ordnance Survey digital map data and geographical information. The mapping data is available to signatories for internal business use, for information services to citizens, in e-mails and in reports and submissions to third parties. Details of the licensing arrangements for the pan-government agreement may be found on the OS website. The licences do not cover the use of data for developing products or reselling the data.

Reproducing OS maps in the media

OS normally charges a royalty for using map extracts in any publication. However, special arrangements have been made to allow newspapers, magazines and television companies to use limited amounts of OS mapping free of charge for the purposes of illustrating editorial matter. The terms and conditions permitting such use are explained in the OS leaflet *Copyright 3 – Reproducing Maps in Newspapers, Magazines and on Television*.

OS business licences

There are two different copyright licences available, depending on the use of OS mapping on websites. The first is a business use licence which allows the unlimited copying of OS mapping for business use and also allows mapping to be placed on a customer's website with no size restrictions, provided the mapping explains and supports the business activities and there is no financial gain involved. Financial gain means selling and obtaining any revenue from advertising or sponsorship. The licence also includes scanning maps to include in an e-mail, but not storing the scanned maps on a database to be used again. The mapping must have some kind of information overlay, e.g. a map extract showing the location of an office (described as any premise where business is conducted) with an arrow indicating the exact location, or it could be highlighted by shading in the area. Mapping, up to A3 in size, may also be used for display and promotion purposes, but the data must contain a background watermark. The purpose of the watermark is not to obscure the mapping but to deter its use for any other purpose. The cost of this licence is based upon the number of offices requiring to be licensed. Costs start at £47.50 plus VAT. This type of licence also includes mapping used in business publications.

If a website contains advertising or sponsorship material, or the owner or controller of the website receives any financial gain, the Ordnance Survey Internet licence is available. The current cost of this licence is £47.50 plus VAT, which allows the use of up to ten 200 cm^2 bitmap images. If any more images of this size are needed, these are charged at a cost of £4.75 plus VAT per image. The licence allows end-users to download and print copies of these images for their own personal use.

There is also a separate licence, available for businesses already licensed, to copy superseded paper maps held by public libraries. Once this licence has been obtained from OS, it may be shown to the public librarian who may give access to the holder. It has to be produced every time. The public librarian is, however, under no obligation to allow access. This would depend on the library access policy but if this is allowed then access must be in accordance with the terms and conditions of the local authority service level agreement.

All copies made under a business licence must carry an acknowledgement specified in the licence to the effect that it is a licensed copy.

A separate licence is available for the publication of paper maps.

OS education licences

Higher and further education establishments (apart from independent, voluntary and LEA schools) have to apply to OS to obtain a licence for any multiple copying from OS mapping. Independent and voluntary schools are granted a free licence to make copies for teaching purposes only. This includes the use of the mapping as a teaching aid or for use in project work.

The licence allows for: the multiple copying for teaching and educational purposes of OS mapping, including the use of digital map data; the use of ten 200 cm^2 bitmap images on the educational establishment's website; and the use of mapping in a brochure or prospectus to show the location of the educational establishment. In higher education, the licence permits copying mapping, not exceeding A3 in size, for the purposes of disseminating academic research, as long as it is acknowledged and is disseminated freely in the public domain, i.e. not published in the normal sense and subject to a charge.

Unless covered by an additional licence, this licence does not allow the sale or distribution of any mapping outside the organization, or digitizing, scanning or storing mapping on a computer.

LEA schools may copy for educational purposes under the local authority SLA (see below) from OS mapping which has been legitimately obtained. This may be done on the premises or by an outside contracted printer. Schools may also obtain copies from the OS mapping held in the public library under this licence. There are no size restrictions when supplying large-scale maps (i.e. 1:10000, 1:2500 or 1:1250 scales). However, at small scales (1:25000 and smaller) copies must not exceed A4 size. It is advisable to contact the public library in advance in order to make it clear that the copying is for educational purposes under the terms of the licence. Otherwise, public libraries are obliged to limit the copying to fair-dealing amounts. If the copying is for a purpose other than educational, i.e. copying for inclusion in a prospectus, then an extra licence for business must be obtained from OS.

Local authority service level agreement

This is a contract between local authorities and the OS to provide mapping. Under this agreement there are strict conditions on where copying may take place. Apart from the copying for educational purposes for publicly funded schools as described above, no public library is allowed to permit copying from OS mapping for purposes other than for fair-dealing purposes. For example, members of the public (private individuals or business persons) may not obtain map copies from the public library for planning applications. These have to be purchased either from the relevant planning department within the local authority (provided it operates a map returns scheme to produce map extracts for this purpose), or from designated Ordnance Survey agents.

Under the SLA, copies made for this purpose under fair dealing or the library regulations may be made only in the public library. They may not be made in other local authority departments. Copies should, ideally, be stamped or labelled *Fair Dealing Copy*. Copying from digital mapping in a public library is dealt with in the same way as printed mapping, i.e. marked 'fair dealing' or with the source acknowledged and the requester should sign a declaration form.

Music licensing for visually impaired persons

At the time of writing (October 2003), the Music Publishers Association was about to introduce a scheme for the multiple copying of printed music for visually impaired persons. The licence conditions are likely to follow the restrictions on making multiple copies under the Copyright (Visually Impaired Persons) Act 2002 which amended the Copyright, Designs and Patents Act 1988 (s. 31B) (see Chapter 2, pages 31–3).

Off-air recording licensing schemes

There are two licensing schemes available to educational establishments only to allow off-air recording of radio and terrestrial television programmes for educational purposes: the licensing scheme from the Educational Recording Agency (ERA) to cover all terrestrial broadcasting with the exception of Open University programmes; the latter only are covered by the Open University Worldwide licensing scheme (see below). Any off-air recording of terrestrial channels must be covered by one or other of these schemes. Both schemes are certified by the Department of Trade and Industry under section 143 of the Act, and are applicable to schools and further and higher education establishments only. At the time of writing satellite and cable channels are not covered by licences. Until they are, off-air recording for educational purposes is allowed (s. 35) (see Chapter 2, page 28). The schemes were last certified in 2003 (see Chapter 10, page 168).

The ERA licence

The bodies which form ERA include: ALCS Ltd, BBC Worldwide Ltd, Channel Four Television Corporation, DACS, the Independent Television Network Ltd, the Mechanical Copyright Protection Society Ltd, Sianel Pedwar Cymru, the Musicians' Union, British Actors Equity Association, the Incorporated Society of Musicians and the British Phonographic Industry Ltd.

Once licensed, the educational establishment may designate individuals to make off-air recordings of radio or TV programmes both in the school and from home. All recordings made under a licence must be labelled with the date and title of each recording, together with a statement to the effect that the recordings may be used only under the terms of the ERA licence. A few licensed educational establishments are required to keep details of every recording made. ERA has the right under the terms of its licence to make inspections of recordings by any licensee. Within the conditions of the licence, tapes may be copied further, used in class, catalogued and kept indefinitely in library collections, and loaned to students within limits. Licensed institutions may also borrow and copy recordings belonging to other ERA licence holders, so if one ERA-licensed educational establishment has forgotten to record a certain programme, it can phone around to similar licensed establishments to obtain a copy. Extracts from recordings may also be used in digitized courseware packages as long as access is on the licensee's premises only. ERA does not permit off-campus access, so no access may be given to distance learning students. The ERA licence may not be used for grabbing film stills for an educational purpose, as the copy made would no longer be a recording but a visual image.

Payment for this licence is according to the type of establishment and the number of FTEs. The tariffs payable are set out in statutory instruments which are changed whenever the scheme is re-certified (currently SI 2003 No. 188). The current fees per FTE range from 23p for primary schools to £1.40 for higher education establishment. However, there are discounted licence fees available for umbrella organizations, e.g. Local Education Authorities.

The Open University licence

The Open University (OU) Off-Air Recording Scheme works differently from the ERA licence. OU programmes are broadcast by the BBC, and the titles of those that are subject to the scheme are published annually by Open University Worldwide Ltd (OUW), previously called Open University Education Enterprises Ltd, and are provided to all licensees in a broadcast calendar. Not all OU programmes, therefore, may be recorded under the scheme.

There are two categories in the scheme: one for schools (primary or secondary), and one for further and higher education establishments. The category for schools allows recordings to be made and retained for teaching purposes until the licence is terminated. The charge for this licence is a small flat-rate fee. The further and higher education licence allows recordings of OU broadcasts to be made, but each recording must be logged and clearly labelled with details of the course, programme number, title and recording date, and submitted to OUW. Payment depends on the total numbers of recordings which are kept for longer than 28 days. So, if after previewing the programme it is erased within 28 days of recording, no fee is charged. For those kept for longer, the fees paid are according to a sliding scale based on the number of recordings held. The more that are held, the lower the unit price charged. No loans for use off the premises are permitted.

It is a condition of the licence that the recordings made may not be edited, cut or amended in any way including by digital manipulation without prior written permission of OUW. Also they must not be shown or disclosed or passed into the possession of any third party or removed from the direct control of the licensee. It goes without saying that recordings must not be exploited in any way either. Details of the scheme including current charges may be found in SI 2003 No. 187.

Under a separate scheme, OUW also licenses establishments which do not fall into the definition of a statutory educational establishment, such as training, educational, medical or professional organizations, both public and private, and commercial establishments, government departments and the armed forces in the UK.

Performance licensing

Permission must be sought from rights holders if a performance is to be public. There are three organizations involved in performance licensing: the Performing Right Society (PRS), Phonographic Performance Ltd (PPL) and Video Performance Ltd.

Playing music in public

PRS is a membership organization working on behalf of composers, lyricists and music publishers. It licenses the public performance and broadcast of copyright works, collects the licence fees, assembles information about the use of that music, and then distributes the royalties. PRS licenses all terrestrial, cable and satellite broadcasters, as well as the use of music on the internet. PRS has over 40 different tariffs for the live or recorded public performance of music in public places such as concert halls, pubs, clubs, factories, offices and aircraft.

An establishment which is considering giving a concert of live copyright-protected music only, i.e. not using sound recordings, will need to have a licence from PRS. The costs for a one-off event are likely to be very modest. However, if an organization is planning to play music sound recordings in public, e.g. at a school disco, an additional licence is needed from PPL. PPL controls the public performance and broadcasting of its members' sound recordings. Members of PPL consist of most of the well-known recording companies, multinationals and independents, as well as a number of specialized repertoire producers. The PPL and PRS will be pleased to discuss individual needs. PPL provides a very useful information sheet.

Playing videos in public

Video Performance Ltd licenses the public performance of videos. This organization should be approached for permission to show any videos in a public setting.

Other available licences

Computer software

When purchasing computer software packages, libraries should consider the appropriate multi-user licence needed. This is non-negotiable. Without such a licence, the software may be loaded onto one machine only.

Licences for downloading and copying music

If music is downloaded, i.e. copied, from the internet, an additional licence to the PRS licence is needed from the Mechanical Copyright Protection Society (MCPS). The copyright holder can also be approached for permission. Like PRS, MCPS is a membership organization which acts on behalf of composers and publishers. It negotiates agreements with those who wish to record music onto many different formats, including CDs, cassettes, videos, audiovisual and broadcast material, and passes the royalties collected on to the appropriate rights holders. MCPS and PRS have formed an operational alliance called the MCPS-PRS Alliance.

HMSO Class Licence

In April 2001 HMSO introduced a Class Licence (sometimes called the click-use licence) intended to complement the Crown copyright waiver. This licence permits anyone to copy from core government material, i.e. material produced by government servants in the practice of their duties. Core material, or core data, is material which has had no added value. Material originating from the trading funds, e.g. Ordnance Survey, would not be covered, nor would personal and security data, any third-party copyrights and any material with value added. The Class Licence is free and is aimed at publishers, companies, schools, universities, local authorities, individuals and of course, libraries – in fact any potential users and re-users of Crown copyright core material. It is renewable after five years. HMSO encourages all organizations wishing to use such material to sign up. Details of how to obtain a Class Licence may be found in Chapter 10, page 170.

Collective worship licensing schemes

Christian Copyright Licensing International (CCLI) can license schools as well as churches and Christian organizations to make copies of copyright hymns and songs of worship. CCLI also offers a music reproduction licence to cover the photocopying of music books, although this does not cover all church-music book publishers. Licences are renewable on an annual basis and currently cost from £57 upwards, depending on the size of the registered school. See their website, given in Appendix C (page 178) for details of their various schemes.

Ten things to remember from this chapter

- the UK government encourages licensing schemes
- some licensing schemes have to be certified, others not
- licensing schemes are monopolies
- having a licence should make operation of an information service easier
- licensing organizations collect money on behalf of authors and rights holders
- there are licensing schemes for most copying and related uses
- licences should offer an indemnity against accusations of infringement
- licensing organizations can enforce compliance, and issue writs on behalf of their members
- rights holders are still concerned about digital copying
- some licences are blanket schemes and some transactional.

7 Infringement, liability, disputes and case law

In this chapter you will learn about:

▓ the meaning of infringement
▓ how to avoid liability
▓ the importance of having a copyright policy
▓ the Copyright Tribunal
▓ some important disputes and relevant case law.

Infringement

Although it is highly unlikely that an information professional will be accused of copyright infringement, there is a need to be aware of what infringement means in order to assess risks. Arguably risks have increased following the Copyright Directive changes, so information professionals will need to be even more careful about their services to users.

Primary infringement (ss. 17–21)

It is an infringement if someone contravenes any of the economic rights, described in Chapter 1, pages 1–3, belonging to the holder(s) of the rights in a work. This is usually referred to as *primary infringement*. For example, making unauthorized copies of a work and selling them without paying a penny to the rights holders would be seen as deliberate copyright infringement for economic gain (piracy). Anyone who authorizes another to commit primary infringement is also liable.

Infringement can occur only if the whole or a 'substantial part' is involved. However, although undefined in the Act, this has been established by case law as turning upon significance of content as well as extent. Therefore almost anything could be judged *substantial* in particular circumstances. For example, copying a two-page summary and recommendations of a 100 page report may be judged substantial in certain cases; copying a few facts from a database may be seen as substantial if they are significant. Similarly, copying a segment of a photograph or a detail from some other form of artistic work may also be regarded as a 'substantial part'. Only a court of law can make these judgements, and this is usually done case by case. *Substantial* is never likely to have a reliably precise definition.

A substantial part may also depend on skill and originality. Although there is no copyright in an idea, if, in producing a new work for commercial publication, an author makes (unacknowledged) excessive use of someone else's written ideas, the author may be accused of infringement even though none of it was actually reproduced. In a dispute, it would be up to the court of law to decide how much skill and originality was used by the author.

Secondary infringement

In addition to primary infringement, certain other acts performed without the consent of the rights holder but done by someone knowing or having reason to believe they would be infringing may be classed as *secondary infringements*.

An important point to note is that a copy made for a purpose allowed under the Act, e.g. under an exception, can automatically become an infringing copy if used in other circumstances. For example, a copy quite legitimately made for an examination question could become an infringing copy if it is 'dealt with', or a photocopy made by a librarian where the librarian knew, or had reason to believe, that the declaration was false could also be an infringing copy.

Importing infringing copies (s. 22)

The Act says that unless specific permission is granted, it is not permitted to import infringing copies into the UK (other than for private or domestic use).

Possessing or dealing with infringing copies (s. 23)

It is illegal to possess in the course of business, sell, hire (or offer to do so), exhibit in public or otherwise distribute infringing copies to such an extent that rights holders' interests are damaged.

Providing the means to make infringing copies (s. 24)

It is an infringement to provide the means specifically designed for making infringing copies, if it is known (or there is a reason to believe) that it will be used to make infringing copies. An example would be a set of printing plates to print banknotes. However, it could also have implications for information professionals if they are aware that infringing copies are made on the library photocopier. See 'Avoiding liability' below.

Without the licence of the copyright owner, it is an infringement to transmit a work by means of a telecommunications system (otherwise than by communication to the public) knowing or having reason to believe that infringing copies of the work will be made by the recipients of the transmission.

Premises used for infringing performance (s. 25)

A person who allows their premises to be used for an infringing public performance of a copyright literary, dramatic or musical work may also be liable for infringement, unless there are grounds for believing that the performance will not infringe.

Provision of apparatus for infringing performance (s. 26)

Anyone who provides apparatus or equipment to assist an infringing performance or the playing of sound recordings, showing of films or receiving visual images or sounds conveyed by electronic means, e.g. downloading music, may also be liable for secondary infringement if such persons are aware that the performances would infringe.

Injunctions against service providers (s. 97A)

This is a new section introduced by the Electronic Commerce (EC Directive) Regulations 2002 (SI 2002 No. 2013) which has important considerations for service providers. The definition of service provider is 'any natural or legal person providing an Information Society service', and the definition of an information society service is 'Any service normally provided for remuneration, at a distance, by means of electronic equipment for the processing (including digital compression) and storage of data, and at the individual request of a recipient of a service.' This could include a library or information provider running a service for profit, e.g. distance learning.

Section 97A states that the 'High Court (in Scotland, the Court of Session) shall have power to grant an injunction against a service provider, where that service provider has actual knowledge of another person using their service to infringe copyright.' Actual knowledge depends on whether the service provider has been made aware of such an infringement and is obliged to act upon it to deal with the infringement. Conversely, if a service provider does not have actual knowledge then there can be no injunction made. It is important, therefore, that service providers act promptly if they are made aware of any infringing material being provided on their network.

Other forms of infringement
Passing off

There are other related forms of infringement. Passing off is one example where someone will pass off their own work as the work of another. This could be painting an artistic work in the style of another with the intention of profiting by the deception.

Sometimes schoolchildren copy artistic works, for example, a cartoon character. The cartoon character is likely to be protected by design right as well as copyright but unless the child tried to profit by the copy, this would not be seen as infringement. Also art students and enthusiasts often make copies of paintings in art galleries. Whether this is acceptable depends again on whether there was intention to pass off and make a profit. Apart from expert forgers, the likelihood of making an exact copy is very small so the resulting works may not be judged to have originality. In any case, the gallery would probably only allow this practice if the works were in the public domain, i.e. out of copyright.

Plagiarism

Plagiarism is another form of infringement and is related to passing off. This is where the work or substantial parts of a work are copied and included in another work without acknowledging the author(s). This may happen in higher and further education where students are using the internet to cheat by downloading essays and other coursework, but sometimes well-known authors are caught out plagiarizing the plots from other works.

Remedies for infringement (ss. 101-115)

Copyright owners are able to protect their rights through civil as well as criminal courts depending on the seriousness of the infringement. The exclusive licensee of the owner of the copyright has since 31 October 2003 also been given the powers to sue (s. 101A). The police or local trading standards officers can also initiate proceedings. Proceedings may take place against alleged infringement in the Magistrates' Courts or the High Court (or the Court of Session in Scotland). The choice will depend on the seriousness of the infringement and how quickly an infringer must be dealt with. If civil proceedings are issued, a rights holder has more control and may act quickly. The drawback from their point of view is that they have to fund the proceedings.

The most likely penalties for minor infringements are: (a) an injunction to prevent further infringement; (b) an instruction to 'deliver up' infringing copies to the rights holders; and (c) the award of damages. This could be an amount equivalent to the profits the rights holder would otherwise have made on sales of any infringing copies. Similar penalties and procedures apply under Scottish law. However, for more damaging infringements, e.g. piracy or communicating a work to the public, a term of imprisonment from anything from 3 months to 2 years may be imposed.

Where an offence committed by a body corporate is proved to have been committed with the consent or connivance of a director, manager, secretary or other similar officer of the body, or a person purporting to act in that capacity, they are guilty of the offence and liable to be proceeded against and punished (s. 110).

New EU proposals on harmonizing penalties for infringement

A new EU directive, Proposal for a Directive of the European Parliament and of the Council on Measures and Procedures to Ensure the Enforcement of Intellectual Property Rights, is progressing through the European Parliament. If adopted, this will give greater power to content owners to enforce their rights for any infringement committed for commercial purposes or indeed for infringements that cause significant harm. The latter could be dangerous, as arguably every alleged infringement could be judged by rights holders to cause harm. In addition there would be new criminal and civil liabilities for third parties which would mean that even if a person has no knowledge of the infringing activity or had no intent to infringe, they still could be liable. This draft directive is being monitored by LACA (see Chapter 10, page 164).

The copyright police

There is no single body which is likely to patrol the library to make sure that information professionals and their users are keeping to the right side of the law. However, some rights holders' representative bodies do act in this way. The CLA, for example, can enter premises to ensure that its licensing conditions are not breached and will not hesitate to take steps to find evidence of copyright infringement. (See page 130 for an example.)

Anecdotal evidence suggests that agents provocateurs representing rights holders (mainly printed matter) have been known to enter public libraries to try to trap unsuspecting library assistants by asking them if they can photocopy substantial amounts.

Major software development companies, concerned about illegal copies of their software, formed the Federation Against Software Theft (FAST) and the Business Software Alliance (BSA) to chase up offenders. The use of unlicensed software can be a civil or criminal offence. Every time unlicensed software is run, an infringement takes place. The Business Software Alliance is also extremely active in this area. Without prior warning, premises which are suspected of holding or using illegal software can be raided. Criminal proceedings can be started leading to hefty damages. Several companies have been prosecuted successfully.

Currently the music and film industries are grabbing the headlines with threats against those who illegally download music and films using file-sharing networks. It is likely that the EU Directive described above will assist in giving them the additional power to search the networks without warning and to prosecute likely offenders.

Avoiding liability

Information professionals are still potentially liable to be accused of infringement. They manage collections of works in copyright and allow access by users. They provide the means for copies to be made. They operate document supply services for users both in-house and outside. They provide access to databases and websites both on-site and off-site. They lend copyright-protected works. Libraries and information units are sometimes seen as the place to go for advice on copyright. They are, in effect, in the middle between protecting the interests of rights holders and satisfying the needs of their users, and may face criticism from both sides. Rights holders may be suspicious of some of the services offered in libraries, e.g. interlibrary document supply. Information professionals, trying hard to ensure that infringements do not occur on their premises, may be accused by users of being obstructive. When managing copyright, information professionals may never win. Nevertheless, they still have to make an effort to ensure compliance. They are part of a recognized profession and as such have to act professionally if they are not to be seen as encouraging copyright infringement or being negligent. Steps have to be taken, therefore, to mitigate any liability.

In the unfortunate event that an accusation of copyright infringement occurs and the case ends up in court, professional conduct would be examined in the judgement. It is important therefore that every effort is made to instil respect and compliance for copyright in staff and users. Some practical suggestions are given below. On the plus side, the profession is recognized by rights holders and the Government (Patent Office) as being the most copyright-compliant because it takes copyright seriously.

Copying machines

The responsibility for any copying or scanning machine within the library premises or information unit rests with the library/information professional in charge. Any infringement which occurs on one of machines could involve the library staff and the organization if a case were brought to court. In any case, just having any form of machine which makes copies could be seen as encouraging illicit copying. This is not the view of CILIP, however, or any of the other information professional organizations, and to date the provision of such copiers in libraries has never been subject to a challenge of secondary infringement. However, to make absolutely sure that librarians and other information staff are not accused of secondary infringement, some precautions should be taken. It is advised, therefore, that prominent notices should be displayed alongside the photocopier or scanner or any other machine which is capable of making copies of protected material. They should be placed in a position such that users will find them difficult to ignore. The notices should make it clear that copyright is protected by law and what limits may be applied, and should advise users to ask staff for guidance when in doubt. (Laminated posters for placing on photocopiers/scanners and for downloading can be bought from CILIP; see details in Chapter 10, pages 165–6, under CILIP).

Users in public libraries

Users are responsible for their own actions. Intervening and challenging a member of the public could be fraught with difficulty. It is a matter of internal policy whether library staff should intervene if they observe apparent infringements but the view of CILIP is that the appropriate member(s) of staff should be informed and any action taken should be as outlined in library policy (see below for advice on library copyright policy).

Information invoking a respect for copyright should be incorporated in publicity material or library/information unit user guides and in any library-use regulations.

Students

Students are also responsible for their own actions. Students are also notorious for bending copyright restrictions. In order to mitigate any liability, it is important that students are made aware of copyright and that they sign to this effect when they join the library or even the educational organization. User education and/or induction programmes should stress the need to respect copyright.

Staff

Staff training programmes should cover copyright in order that all staff are aware of the need to respect it and the limits of copying. Line managers responsible for library and information resources should be included in such programmes.

Management should consider cautionary statements in staff conditions of service and library conditions of access. If staff infringe, the ultimate responsibility rests with the top person responsible for the actions of employees. However, having a licence does (or should) provide indemnity for copying as part of compliance with its terms.

The importance of a copyright policy

It helps, and is good practice within an organization, especially a large one, to have a copyright policy in place, giving details of any permissions or licences and whether the organization may safely take advantage of copying under a permitted exception. It also helps to ensure that all those concerned are following the same rules. As has been seen, the law is vague about definitions and limits on copying, and one can never really be sure that what is being copied is not going to be the subject of litigation. If all library and information staff are following the same policy, one has a greater sense of security.

To begin with, it is obviously extremely important that at least a basic knowledge of copyright law is obtained before formulating such a copyright policy. Inadequate knowledge could mean that management might ignore potential high risks or, conversely, be so worried that staff and users are told not to copy anything. For example, giving a user the green light to burn music downloaded from the internet would be unprofessional and might result in a nasty court case. Conversely, banning all copying from newspapers because the Newspaper Licensing Agency has said that your organization must be licensed if items are copied from newspapers is equally unprofessional and unhelpful to users, and shows ignorance of statutory permitted uses such as fair dealing.

The next step should be to examine potential risks by undertaking a copyright audit. What copying requirements are there? Where are the photocopiers, scanners, computers? What is copied, where is it done and by whom? Can one see what is going on?

Is such copying authorized? If yes, under what authority? Are there conditions? What are the limits? If not, how high are the risks? Is there a compliance solution? Answering such questions will help to formulate guidance as well as finding solutions to compliance problems. It is also advisable in such a policy to give guidance to staff on how to handle queries about copyright and related issues, so as not to put the organization at risk. It is important that staff have the necessary knowledge to be able to handle any queries, and if not, to know where to find it. Any unauthorized copying should be brought to the attention of management, and a decision can be made whether to cease such copying or obtain the necessary permissions or licences. In any case, those who are regularly making and supplying copies of copyright material outside that which is permitted under a statutory exception (e.g. fair dealing, the library regulations, judicial proceedings, etc.) are advised to apply for a licence. See Chapter 6 for details of licensing schemes available.

A copyright policy is also essential for managing the rights which an organization may hold, either as the original creators of the material or because they have acquired them through donation or some other means. For example, educational establishments often create original teaching material, or a local studies library may acquire a collection of unpublished documents. If there are copyrights in 'home-grown documents' then knowledge of what this means and what may be exploited is essential. For example: who actually owns the copyright – individuals or the organization? Will the rights be used to make money for the organization or will the copyrights be waived? Under what conditions will this happen? What will be the policy on access? And so on.

IFPI, the international organization representing the phonographic industry, has produced a copyright guide for academic institutions which includes some suggested wording for a copyright policy document – obviously with the accent on the illegality and liability of downloading recorded music and file sharing by students. The guide may be found at www.ifpi.org/site-content/library/academic-brochure-english.pdf.

The Copyright Tribunal (ss. 145–52)

An important feature of the Act was the establishment of a Copyright Tribunal to arbitrate on the terms and conditions of licensing schemes. Members of the Tribunal are mainly lawyers and civil servants, plus a few ordinary members who are recruited from time to time. The ordinary members' posts demand appropriate skills, but above all sound common sense. Details of the Tribunal rules of operation are in SI 1992 No. 467. These may also be found on the Patent Office website. The Tribunal deals with several aspects of licensing disputes.

Anyone with a grievance regarding a licensing scheme may apply to the Copyright Tribunal. This may be about the terms of an existing licence or one that is in the process of being negotiated. The Tribunal has the power to vary terms and impose fees. One can also apply to the Tribunal if a licensing organization unreasonably refuses to grant a licence. Reference to the Tribunal should not necessarily mean excessive costs will be incurred, although this has been the general perception until recently. The higher education sector took the CLA to the Copyright Tribunal (see pages 131–2).

Circumvention of technical protection systems and rights management systems

These were two of the new rights included in the EU Copyright Directive. The Copyright and Related Rights Regulations 2003 subsequently had to introduce a completely new section to the Act on the rules regarding protection against the circumvention of technical protection measures or systems (TPMs). The umbrella terms are called the Electronic Copyright Management Systems (ECMS) or Digital Rights Management Systems (DRMS). These are management systems software designed to enable trading or usage of works in electronic form in a regulated manner. This could be by preventing unauthorized access and/or monitoring usage and distribution, e.g. using watermarking, digital identification or other means. Thus, works are not only protected by the law against acts of infringement, they could also be protected by ECMS and by a law to protect the ECMS from circumvention!

This has implications for users authorized by statute who may wish to access such works under a statutory permission and are prevented from doing so because of the TPM. User groups lobbied heavily in Brussels to make this point when the Copyright Directive was under discussion (see Chapter 8, pages 147–8). Eventually, a compromise was agreed which allowed member states to put safeguards or remedies in place to ensure that beneficiaries of a statutory exception may continue to benefit. These are described below.

Technical protection systems

It is an infringement to circumvent a technical device applied to a computer program (s. 296) and similarly it is an infringement to circumvent a technical device applied to works other than computer programs (s. 296ZA). It is also an offence to traffic in such equipment; to manufacture for sale or hire equipment which is primarily designed to circumvent or facilitate the circumvention; to import (other than for domestic use) such equipment; or in the course of business to sell or let for hire, offer or expose for hire, advertise for sale or hire, possess, distribute otherwise than in the course of a business to such an extent as to affect prejudicially the copyright owner (s. 296ZB).

Remedies where technological measures prevent permitted acts (s. 296ZE)

The Act says that:

> Where the application of any effective technological measure to a copyright work other than a computer program prevents a person from carrying out a permitted act in relation to that work then that person or a person being a representative of a class

of persons prevented from carrying out a permitted act may issue a notice of complaint to the Secretary of State.

This means that a user or a representative of that user may complain to the Secretary of State if they are unable to carry out any of the exceptions listed in Chapter 2. An example could be a person wishing to download a copy from a website for the purposes of judicial proceedings but who is prevented from doing so by a TPM. The Secretary of State then has to investigate to see whether the complaint is upheld by checking that there is no voluntary or contractual agreement in place between the rights holders and the users. A complaint would be invalid if works are made available 'on agreed contractual terms in such a way that members of the public may access them from a place and at a time individually chosen by them'. It would not apply, for example, to works made available from a subscription database such as an e-journal, or to on-demand television programmes which can be available when required.

If the complaint is upheld, then the Secretary of State is empowered only to *direct* that the rights holder provides a remedy to enable the user to benefit from the exception. If this direction is ignored, the applicant's only redress would be to take the offender to court, as the Secretary of State cannot enforce this direction. All the Government can do is to name and shame the offender. This is not totally satisfactory, as it is likely to discourage many complaints from individual users. Another drawback is that, with regard to websites operating outside the UK, any ruling is likely to be unenforceable. The regulations (directions) on the necessary procedures for the complaint and its remedy will be published in more detail by the Secretary of State in due course.

Rights management systems (s. 296ZG)

Rights management information 'means any information . . . which identifies the work, the author, the copyright owner or the holder of any intellectual property rights, or information about the terms and conditions of use of the work, and any numbers or codes that represent such information'. Similar to the protection of technical measures, protection against circumvention of rights management information is also given to copyright owners. It is an infringement, therefore, to remove or alter electronic rights management information knowingly and without authorization. Also, if works which have had rights management information removed or altered are distributed, imported for distribution or communicated to the public, this is also an offence if the person committing these acts is aware of the infringement.

Disputes and case law

Most of the disputes about copyright are settled out of court, so there are not that many cases relevant to information professionals, though there are several which are on the fringes and do, or may, have some bearing on information service practices. In any case they are interesting and worth noting. Some of the examples given below are from outside the UK. Information has been gleaned from several sources, not necessarily from legal reports.

Copying images

In a case in New York, the Bridgeman Art Library sued the Canadian company Corel for copying images which Bridgeman claimed belonged to it. These images were photographic transparencies of works of art in the public domain. The alleged infringements occurred in the USA, Canada and Great Britain. Despite Bridgeman having registered these images in the US as derivative works, Corel contested that Bridgeman had no valid copyright and that there was no evidence of copying. Most of the original works of art are owned by museums in the UK and the photographs were first published in the UK, so the applicable law was decided to be that of the UK.

The crucial question was whether there was enough skill, judgement and labour expended to qualify these images for protection. This principle is exemplified in the observation by the Privy Council which states:

> It takes great skill, judgement and labour to produce a good copy by painting or to produce an enlarged photograph from a positive print . . . no-one would reasonably contend that the copy painting or enlargement was an 'original' artistic work in which the copier is entitled to claim copyright. Skill, labour or judgement merely in the process of copying cannot confer originality . . . . There must in addition be some element of material alteration or embellishment which suffices to make the totality of the work an original work.

On this basis it was judged that the images did not qualify for copyright protection under the UK Act as there was no evidence of embellishment or alteration to the works. The judge could not be persuaded either that there was originality in the photographic works. In this case the works were akin to a scientific process. The case was dismissed. (1998 US Dist. LEXIS 17920, SDNY, 13 November 1998.)

In 1999 the family of the artist Henri Matisse won a landmark case over royalties. Phaidon Press, a publisher of coffee-table books, had used images of the artist in these books claiming that it copied them under the statutory copyright exception for criticism or review, and so did not have to pay to use them. This was disputed, and Phaidon was forced to pay seven years' lost royalties. (Matisse Estate Wins Payout, *The Times*, 25 August 1999, p. 9.)

Copying books and periodicals

The action familiarly called the Texaco case was an important precedent with implications for profit-based organizations in the early 1990s. (Note: the US *fair use* is not quite the same as the UK's fair dealing). Publishers in the US (American Geophysical Union, Elsevier Science, Pergamon, Springer, Wiley and Academic Press) successfully sued Texaco for photocopying from their books and journals for their staff without permission. In the decision ruled in July 1992, despite the claim by Texaco that its copying was under fair use, the judge ruled that companies cannot copy articles for internal use without first obtaining permission and compensating the rights holders. An appeal was lodged in September 1992 but the ruling was upheld. (Appeals Court Upholds Texaco Copyright Ruling, *The Bookseller*, 11 November 1994.)

The Copyright Licensing Agency, acting on behalf of two publishers, the Open University and Centaur Press, obtained a considerable financial settlement for unauthorized photocopying from Essenheath Ltd – the commercial arm of Greenwich College, an independent business college in London. The CLA hired a private investigator to enrol as a student and found evidence that the college had reproduced copyright material without permission or licence for use in coursework by students. The college was ordered to take out a CLA licence. (Private Investigator Helps CLA Win Settlement, *The Bookseller*, 5 March 1993.)

In 1984 Manchester City Council was ordered to pay £75,000 for copyright infringement. The case was triggered by a supply teacher who was astonished to find quantities of his own book in photocopied form in a school stockroom. (In the Twilight World of the Copyright Busters, *Guardian Education*, 16 March 1993.)

The CLA and four publishers were successful in taking Dar Al Handasah, a firm of engineering consultants, plus two other named defendants to the High Court for infringing copyright in their publications. The case was initiated as part of the Copywatch campaign whereby a former employee 'blew the whistle' on them to the CLA. (CLA news release, December 1996.)

Copying newspapers

In 1999 the NLA successfully sued the retailer Marks & Spencer for making and distributing internally unlicensed copies from newspapers. M&S internal press offices obtained cuttings relevant to M&S from a cuttings agency, copied the cuttings and distributed them to a restricted list of executives and directors who needed the information for a variety of company purposes. M&S used the defence of fair dealing for news reporting, which of course does not cover the typographical arrangement. Mr Justice Lightman decided in the High Court that each newspaper article copied had its own typographical arrangement copyright, and the retailer's copying of those articles was not 'fair dealing for the purpose of reporting current events'. In an interesting twist when the case went to the Court of Appeal in May 2000, the decision was reversed, it being found that Marks & Spencer did not infringe copyright in typographical arrangements of published editions by copying and distributing press cuttings. The Court of Appeal decided that the term 'typographical arrangement' refers to the typographical arrangement of a whole newspaper, not of each individual item. The individual cuttings copied by M&S were not therefore substantial parts of the whole newspapers from which they were taken, and so there was no infringement of copyright. This decision was upheld by the House of Lords where it was judged that the protection for the typographical arrangement was for the *whole* of a publication, not separate parts: 'a given typographical arrangement might be protected if published alone but not amount to a substantial part of a published edition of a larger work into which it was incorporated'. (Circulating Press Cuttings Went Beyond Fair Dealing, *The Times*, 26 January 1999, p. 4; No Breach in Copying Cutting, *Times Law Reports*, 13 July 2001; *Newspaper Licensing Agency* v. *Marks and Spencer plc*, 12 July 2001 [2001] UKHL 38.)

Licensing disputes

In July 2000 the Copyright Tribunal was invoked in the dispute over the licence renewal negotiations between the Committee of Vice-Chancellors and Principals (CVCP) – later renamed Universities UK (UUK) – representing the higher education sector, and the CLA and DACS. The dispute arose because there were widespread concerns over the terms of the previous (1998) licence, as well as the fact that the CLA had imposed non-negotiated extra charges and conditions during the licence term following on from the agreement with DACS to include artistic works in their repertoire. In September 2001 the Copyright Tribunal convened a hearing where both sides put forward their views. This was accompanied by a vast amount of 'evidence'. The UUK team stressed the difficulties, extra costs and administrative burden of having to clear rights to make course packs through CLARCS. The CLA wished to keep the conditions and to increase fees.

An interim decision was made by the Tribunal in December 2001 pending finalization of the new HE licence terms between the two parties. These were agreed in the following March. The main changes were: the making of study (course) packs was allowed in the basic licence, so CLARCS clearance was no longer necessary; the cost of the licence was set at £4 for each FTE; payment was to increase in line with the retail price index increase on an annual basis; the calculation of the royalty was to be based on the number of FTEs and not on any 'notional number of pages or price per page'; and artistic works were to be included in the basic licence. The revised terms of the scheme were back-dated to 1 August 2001, and the licence runs for five years from that date. Because CLARCS was no longer needed for the clearance of course packs, the CLA said that it would be phased out. The Copyright Tribunal ruled that the CLA had to meet costs of more than £1m, including a quarter of UUK's total costs of £800,000.

The Tribunal made interesting and valid comments about the excessive amounts of paper produced (24 lever-arch files of materials) and the excessive costs incurred by both sides. The interim report indicated that the Tribunal 'must be accessible at reasonable cost' and that it was disappointed that reference to the Tribunal was seen 'as a last resort: a failure of a most serious kind' in the licence negotiations. The Tribunal 'exists at least in part to prevent unreasonable terms being imposed on licensees who have little choice but to take a licence'. Licensees perceived that application to the Tribunal was far too complex and lengthy, and that the costs were prohibitive. If the Tribunal was out of their league, licensees had no option but to accept unreasonable terms. Licensees, therefore, can deduce from this that reference to the Tribunal need not be expensive, and should not be considered a last resort but a genuine option in any negotiations. This was very positive comment. (CLA news release, 13 December 2001, accessed on CLA website; UUK news release, 13 December 2001, accessed on UUK website; Tribunal decision on Patent Office website; UUK Scores Victory in Copyright Battle, *Times Higher Education Supplement*, 21 December 2001, p. 6.)

Hypertext linking

The *Shetland Times* brought a case against a fellow online newspaper, *Shetland News*, for providing direct hypertext links to news items on its site and so bypassing its homepage. Readers of *Shetland News* were unaware that they were reading items from *Shetland Times*. The *Shetland Times* based its case on hypertext links being a breach of copyright. In November 1997 the case was settled out of court, but *Shetland News* was ordered to acknowledge all links. (Shetland Settlement Fails to Defuse Row, *Press Gazette*, 21 November 1997, p. 10; *Shetland Times Ltd v. Dr Jonathan Wills and Another* (1996) S.C.L.R. 160; J. P. Connolly and S. Cameron, Fair Dealing in Webbed Links of Shetland Yarns, *Journal of Information Law and Technology*, no. 2, 1998, http://elj.warwick.ac.uk/jilt).

In Germany an online recruitment company, StepStone, successfully obtained an injunction against a rival company from linking to its web pages. The argument was similar to the Shetland case in that the rival was bypassing StepStone's home page and therefore its advertising potential. (Online Recruiter Wins Ban on Rival's Weblinks, *Financial Times*, 17 Janurary 2001, p. 4.)

In the Netherlands, in the case of *PCN v. Kranten.com*, Kranten.com used headlines from PCN articles to link to the PCN website which displayed the full news article. When PCN claimed a breach of copyright and database right and sought an injunction to stop Kranten.com using these deep links, the injunction was refused. As Dutch copyright law allowed the copying of the headlines, as long as the source is identified, there was no infringement of copyright, and the court decided that database right was not infringed either, as there is no database right in a headline. Interestingly, it was judged that deep links did not actually prevent access to the home page and the potential for advertising revenue, and, in any case, PCN should have considered this when making the decision about where its advertising was to be placed. (Coombes, 2001, see Chapter 10, page 170.)

Haymarket, the publisher, started legal action in 2000 against Burmah Castrol alleging 'calculated and blatant infringement of its online intellectual property rights'. Haymarket's complaint concerned links on Castrol's website which 'frame' content from two of the publisher's sites, whatcar.com and autosport.com, within a Castrol-branded border. Haymarket alleged that Castrol never sought permission to use its website material. The publisher claimed breach of copyright, as well as alleged passing off on the basis that the framing suggested that the Castrol sites are associated with it. Haymarket was willing to let third parties use its branded content 'assuming that the right commercial arrangements were put in place'. In 2002 the US courts dismissed a case brought by Ticketmaster against Tickets.com over deep linking – providing a route to another company's website which bypasses the home page and so may affect advertising revenues. (Publisher Sues over Web Link, *Financial Times*, 10 January 2001, p. 3; How Far Does Copyright Extend in Cyberspace? *Financial Times*, 15 January 2001, p. 18.)

Crown copyright

An American website was publishing tide times for the US, parts of Europe and Japan and was receiving more than 6500 requests per month from users for UK data. The administrator of the site was told by the UK Hydrographic Office that this was a contravention of Crown copyright and the information must be removed. (Tide Publisher Makes Waves with Queen, *Daily Telegraph, Dotcom Telegraph*, p. 2E, 1 March 2001.)

The Automobile Association admitted to plagiarizing the Ordnance Survey by passing the latter's maps off as its own. In an out-of-court settlement, it agreed to pay £20m in compensation. The previous year the AA agreed to pay £875,000 for breaching copyright of 64 maps. The OS was able to prove copying because it included tiny errors in its own maps. (AA to Pay £20m for Copying Road Maps, *The Independent*, 6 March 2001, p. 12; Copying Ordnance Survey Maps Costs AA £20m, *The Guardian*, 6 March 2001, p. 1; Mapping the AA's Decline from League of Gentlemen to Copy Clerks, *The Times*, 7 March 2001, p. 22; AA Caught Mapping, *The Bookseller*, 9 March 2001, p. 5.)

Electoral registers

Although the court case described below is not exactly a copyright case, it is included because it is a landmark ruling and has direct implications for access to registers in public libraries. (See Chapter 4, page 67 for implications.)

The case was between a member of the public, Mr Robertson, who refused to allow his personal details to be collected on the Wakefield electoral register because he was aware that his details were being sold to commercial companies for direct-marketing purposes. He claimed initially that this was a violation of his human rights but it was ruled that the relevant legal violation was data privacy. The judge ruled in his favour, saying that although the Representation of the People Act 2000 was not yet in force, the obligations of the EU Directive on Data Privacy were. According to the Information Commissioner, the practice of selling the registers to commercial companies has long been inconsistent with the principles of data protection and conflicts with the right to respect for personal privacy. This ruling has obvious implications for electoral registration officers, who were later advised that electoral registers should cease to be sold to commercial companies or credit reference agencies.

Details of the court case (Queens Bench Division) may be found at http://porch.ccta.gov.uk/courtser/judgements.nsf/ (the date of the case is 16 November 2001 and the claimant is Brian Reid Beetson Robertson). The statement by the Information Commissioner is at www.dataprotection.gov.uk/dpr/dpdoc.nsf (search on <electoral registers>). The Representation of the People Act 2000 is available at www.hmso.gov.uk/acts/acts2000/20000002.htm.

Computer software

The software giants are certainly not soft when it comes to finding illegal software in schools. A local education authority in Philadelphia was ordered by Microsoft to get rid of illegal software in its schools or face multimillion dollar fines. Other school districts in the USA were also forced to audit their software, or else! Behind these campaigns is the Business Software Alliance which is also looking into illegal software in schools in the UK. (Punished for Software Piracy, *Times Educational Supplement*, 3 August 2001, p. 10).

Databases

In the now deemed classic case of *Magill* v. *BBC, Independent Television Publications Ltd and RTE*, the European Commission ruled that the refusal of the television companies to grant Magill licences to produce a guide to TV listings was an abuse of their dominant position under Article 86 of the Treaty of Rome. The Commission found in Magill's favour and made an order for licences to be granted. The TV companies went to the European Court to appeal but the judgment was upheld. (Magill Case Result, *News for EUSIDIC Members*, special edition, April 1995.)

On 9 February 2001 a case was heard between the British Horseracing Board (BHB) and the bookmaker William Hill. The case concerned horse-racing fixtures. The BHB objected to William Hill using information in its internet betting service about race meetings conducted by the BHB. William Hill extracted data without licence from Satellite Information Services Ltd, which held a licence from the BHB to transmit much of the Board's data to its subscribers, and then used the information on its internet betting site. The court found that as William Hill had downloaded substantial amounts of data, the company had therefore infringed database right. Information professionals hoped this case would shed some light on some of the definitions of the terms used in the Database Regulations, but all that was concluded was that any copying of data could be judged substantial if it was seen as useful. What is also interesting is that the presiding judge, Justice Laddie, preferred to base his judgment on the original language of the EU Database Directive rather than that of the implementing Database Regulations. (HC 2000 1335, judgment on 9 February 2001, www.courtservice.gov.uk/judgments/judg_home.htm; Directive Protection for Database Investment, *Times Law Reports*, 23 February 2001, p. 28.)

Technical protection systems

A landmark case concerning the circumvention of technical protection systems took place in the USA in August 2000. It began with a young Norwegian boy, Jon Johansen, who decrypted a protection system on a DVD he had bought because he was unable to play it on his computer, which had a Linux operating system. He wrote some software called DeCSS to crack the code but also made the software available on the internet for others to use for similar purposes. However, it was found that the code could be used to decrypt films as well as

DVDs and so several Hollywood movie studios, fearing widespread piracy of Napster proportions (see below), then sued the owner of website in the USA, because making the code available infringed the US Digital Millennium Copyright Act. Eric Corley, the website owner, also published details in a hackers magazine. The case, brought by the Motion Picture Industry of America, was successful.

In Norway in 2002, the same Jon Johansen was taken to court charged with having decrypted the DVD. However, it was judged that he had done nothing wrong by writing the software in order to enable him to play something which he had bought legally. Also, he had not used the DeCSS for an illegal purpose or contributed to illegal copying . The case was therefore dismissed. It is interesting to note that when Norway updates its law in line with the Copyright Directive provisions, circumvention of a technical protection system will be a criminal offence there as well as in the USA and the UK. (Hollywood Sues Website to Stop Copying of Films, *The Guardian*, 19 July 2000, p. 13; Hollywood Wins Piracy Case over DVD Hacking, *Financial Times*, 18 August 2000, p. 8; Taylor Wessing, *Digital Media Law Update*, 10 and 17 January 2003 [available to subscribers only.])

Downloading and file sharing

In January 2003 the High Court dismissed defences brought by Stelios Haji-Ioannou's company easyInternetcafé over illegal downloading of music at its cybercafés. Customers were paying a £5 fee to download files, some of which included sound recordings, to a server owned by the café. They had been warned about copyright infringement. The defence argued that the downloading was actually performed by customers, and not staff, even though the files could then be burned onto CDs. Mr Haji-Ioannou's defence claimed that users were time-shifting (recording solely for the purpose of viewing or listening at a more convenient time – see Chapter 2, page 35, and that copies made were for private and domestic use. Both these arguments were rejected. Although the easyInternetcafé business was profit-making, the case could have ramifications for non-profit-makers, as it appears that those who offer a downloading service could be responsible for any infringing acts. This could have serious implications, particularly for public libraries, many of which provide CD burners or burn or print off texts from a central server for the customer, who pays on collection. (Net Café Chain Loses Battle over CD Copying, *Financial Times*, 29 January 2003, p. 2; Copyright Infringed by Music Downloads at easyInternetcafé, *The Times*, 29 January 2003, p. 9.)

Representatives of the British record industry have said that they were going to sue universities that allow students to use their computer networks to download music from the internet. Although the universities' response was that it was not their job to police internet use on behalf of the record industry, the BPI and IFPI claim it is in the interest of universities to crack down on illegal copying and introduce filtering software. Downloading clogs up computers and internet bandwidth, and exposes the systems to viruses. (Universities to be Sued over Music Downloads, *The Times*. 28 March 2003, p. 19.)

Napster, the music-sharing internet service, lost a long-running court battle with the Recording Industry Association of America (RIAA) over copyright and was ordered to stop providing illegally copied music recordings in February 2001 and to remove pirated files. However, the battle between the music industry and similar file-sharing services still continues. (Napster Loses Court Fight to Supply Free Music on the Net, *The Guardian*, 13 February 2001, p. 2; The Day Music Died on the Net, *The Times*, 14 February 2001, p. 8; An Infringement Too Far, *Financial Times*, 4 April 2001.)

The RIAA filed copyright infringement lawsuits against four college students accusing them of setting up Napster-like file-swapping services on their campus networks. (Students Accused of Piracy: Record Suit Seeks $150,000 Per Song, *SiliconValley.com*, 4 April 2003, www.siliconvalley.com/mld/siliconvalley/5558442. htm.)

Ten things to remember from this chapter

- a substantial part has to be copied before it is seen to be an infringement
- a substantial part could equally be a question of *what* is copied as well as how much
- information professionals need to be aware that infringing acts could take place on their premises and so could be liable
- users and staff should be made aware of copyright and the consequences of infringement
- notices should be placed near copying equipment
- in-house copyright policies help to give guidance to staff, and identify risks
- the Copyright Tribunal acts as a mediator between licensing organizations and their licensees
- circumvention of, and trafficking in, technical protection systems is illegal
- public librarians should be wary of allowing CD-burning of music in libraries
- the entertainment industry (music, film and software) is the most active in enforcing copyright nationally and internationally.

8   International and European copyright

In this chapter you will learn about:

■ international conventions and trade agreements
■ European Union copyright harmonization
■ what is happening in parts of the rest of the world.

The need to protect authors from the pirating of their works has been around for hundreds of years. In 1710 the Statute of Anne was the first copyright law passed in Great Britain. This gave limited rights to authors to protect their works. In later years, with the growth of international trade and the desire to create markets for copyright works in other countries, authors and, more specifically, their publishers needed assurance that adequate copyright protection would be given for their works wherever they were traded. In 1838 Parliament passed legislation which enabled Great Britain to become a party to international copyright agreements, with the result that bilateral agreements were set up with several European neighbour states. Talks were also begun between the UK and the USA to discuss an Anglo-American copyright agreement, although because Americans feared that any such international agreement would have an adverse effect on their embryonic book trade, this was resisted until as late as 1891. A considerable amount of pirating of published editions by British authors continued until that time. It is well known that Charles Dickens, whose books were affected by piracy, was incensed by this.

The Berne Convention

Modern intellectual property laws are based on rights laid down by international conventions. In 1886 the Berne Convention for the Protection of Literary and Artistic Works was agreed. Eight European nations, including the UK, became signatories to the Convention and became what was called the Berne Union of signatory states.

Berne is considered the most important copyright convention, and the majority of national copyright laws are based on it. Under the terms of this convention, authors are entitled to some basic rights of protection of their intellectual output. The rights laid down by Berne are translated into a set of restrictive acts which only the author, as creator, can authorize. Since 1886 there have been many revisions to Berne, each one increasing the scope of protection. However, not every original signatory signs up to a revision. Some are therefore signatories to one revision and others to another. The current revision is the Paris Act of 1971. The UK is a signatory to all revisions. Most countries in the world, currently 150, have now signed up to the Berne Convention, and others are being forced by international trade laws to at least comply with its principles. See WTO and TRIPS below. (It is interesting to note that the USA did not join Berne until as late as 1989.)

Berne principles

The Berne Convention is based on three principles:

- mutual protection – among Berne Union members, each state must protect the works of others to the same level as in their own countries (principle of national treatment)
- automatic protection – no registration is required before protection is given
- the principle of independent protection – protection is independent of the existence of any protection in the country of origin of the work, except that if the term of protection is longer and the work ceases to be protected in the country of origin, protection may be denied once protection in the country of origin ceases.

Berne also lays down:

- a series of provisions determining the minimum protection to be granted (mainly author's life plus 50 years or, for an anonymous work, 50 years after it has been made available to the public)
- special provisions available to developing countries if they want to make use of them
- a set of rights for authors (reproduction and translation, recitation in public, public performance of dramatic or musical works and communication to the public of such performances, recording of musical works, broadcasting, use in audiovisual works, adaptations and moral rights)
- scope for nations to permit exceptions to these rights.

This latter provision regarding exceptions is important for information professionals and their users. This is covered by the famous Article 9 (2). Under the terms of this article, signatory nations are given the right to grant certain exceptions to the right of reproduction, within limitations: 'It shall be a matter for legislation in the countries of the [Berne] Union to permit the reproduction of such works in certain special cases, provided that such reproduction does not conflict with a normal exploitation of the work and does not unreasonably prejudice the legitimate interests of the author.' This is known familiarly as the Berne three-step test. It is the test that the UK Government applies when considering exceptions and limitations. It is also reinforced (with minor changes) in Article 5.5 of the EU Copyright Directive (2001/29/EC).

The Universal Copyright Convention

Berne is complex, demanding a big commitment on behalf of governments, and originally many countries in both developed and developing nations were unwilling or unable to sign up to all the conditions. In 1952 a compromise was reached between Berne and the various conventions originated by or between the countries of North and South America. This culminated in the Universal Copyright Convention, which was agreed at a UNESCO conference in Geneva.

The main features of UCC are:

- works of a given country must carry a copyright notice to secure protection in other UCC countries – the internationally recognized © copyright symbol
- foreign works must be treated as though they are national works (same as the Berne principle)
- a minimum term of protection – life plus 25 years (not life plus 50, like Berne)
- the author's translation rights may be subjected to compulsory licensing.

Conventions on neighbouring rights

Neighbouring rights, often called related rights, refer to rights for performance and associated rights. There are two neighbouring rights conventions. These complement Berne and UCC, giving protection to performers and producers of audiovisual media. The UK is a signatory to both the following conventions.

The Rome Convention

The International Convention for the Protection of Performing Artists, Producers of Phonograms and Broadcasting Organizations (Rome Convention) 1961 provides for the exclusive right of performers and broadcasters to authorize fixations of their performances and broadcasts respectively, as well as the exclusive right of reproduction for performers, phonogram producers and broadcasting organizations. This convention established the use of the (P) symbol which accompanies the year or date of first publication. However, the Rome Convention has not had a successful history in attracting signatories, as many nations are not able, or have decided it is not in their interest, to comply with its terms.

The Phonogram Convention

The Convention for the Protection of Producers of Phonograms Against Unauthorized Duplication of their Phonograms (Geneva) 1971, familiarly called the Phonogram Convention, prevents unauthorized duplication of phonograms and was an attempt to strengthen the fight against piracy. The fear of piracy is behind many of the strict controls in countries where the phonographic industry is big business. There are many nations with limited protection for copyright works, or where protection does not exist at all, or where piracy is uncontrollable. Because of difficulties abiding by its terms, very few nations acceded to this Convention, much to the regret of phonogram producers.

The WIPO and WIPO treaties

The United Nations organization responsible for managing the major international copyright conventions is the World Intellectual Property Organization (WIPO). WIPO is responsible for the promotion of the protection of intellectual property throughout the world through co-operation among states. It runs programmes for development co-operation in copyright and neighbouring rights in developing countries in order to promote respect for copyright, gives technical assistance and also helps in setting up collecting societies to collect royalty payments. Obviously one of the main objectives of WIPO is to encourage all countries to fall in line with the latest revisions of the main copyright conventions. The WIPO website contains regularly updated information on all its conventions and their signatories. The interests of the library and information professions are regularly looked after in WIPO by IFLA and EBLIDA (see Chapter 10, pages 166–7).

The WIPO Standing Committee of Experts

During the 1990s the WIPO Standing Committees of Experts debated a possible Protocol to the Berne Convention. A parallel committee also discussed a proposal for a new instrument (treaty) to give stronger protection to performers and producers of phonograms to update the Rome and Phonogram conventions, and so hopefully make protection more acceptable to more nations. There was also growing pressure for WIPO to help resolve the problems caused by the impact of digital technology. In May 1996 the WIPO discussions were concluded with the preparation of three treaties to be debated at a diplomatic conference in December 1996. Many of the new rights contained in TRIPS (see below), such as protection for computer programs, compilations of data, and rental right, were incorporated into the WIPO proposals.

International protection for databases

The committee of experts, renamed the Standing Committee on Copyright and Related Rights, still meets regularly. Several issues have been considered by the Standing Committee, including the protection of databases. Proposals have been put forward which are similar to those in the controversial EU Directive on the legal protection for databases (96/9/EC) which gives a separate protection for non-original databases. It is not surprising that only the European countries support the idea fully, as they have more to protect. Countries which are still in the process of development are mostly against it. The main concern of these countries is for the protection of expressions of folklore. Because of this division, WIPO commissioned an economic study of protection of databases to see whether protection is necessary. There still appears to be much reluctance in adopting a new instrument.

WIPO treaties

At the diplomatic conference in December 1996, proposals for three new copyright treaties were received and discussed. These were drafted jointly by the European Commission and the USA and immediately became controversial for the user community and intermediaries. Although author and performer rights were being made much stronger, it was at the expense of having adequate user privileges. The three treaties on the table for adoption were: on copyright, on performers' and phonogram producers' rights and on the protection of databases. However, because of lack of time (and maybe inclination) the discussion on databases was deferred and is still the subject of discussion at the WIPO Standing Committee (see above).

As well as strengthening the rights of performers and record producers, there were new rights added in the proposed instruments. Among these were: a new definition of the reproduction right to include all temporary and incidental copies (adopted as an agreed statement rather than a right); a communication to the public right to prohibit unauthorized transmission by any telecommunication method (agreed); and legal protection against circumvention for digital rights management systems (agreed). It will be noted that all these are included in the EU Copyright Directive (2001/29/EC) – see below.

Because of a strong lobby by consumer groups, among them IFLA and EBL-

IDA, provision was included in these treaties for signatory nations to allow new exceptions and limitations in their copyright laws which are appropriate to the digital environment, as well as affirming that existing exceptions applied to both the print and electronic environment. There were agreed statements to this effect.

At the end of the conference, the WIPO Copyright Treaty (WCT) and the WIPO Performers and Producers of Phonograms Treaty (WPPT) were both adopted. These are often referred to as the internet treaties as they addressed the issues surrounding protection for works on the internet. They are seen as a continuation of the Berne Convention, and the links to Berne are made clear in the text. The treaties also comply with the obligations under TRIPS (see below). Before the treaties could enter into force, at least 30 signatory nations had to implement the new provisions into their own laws. Both treaties have now been ratified, although until all EU member states implement the provisions of the Copyright Directive (2001/29/EC), the EU cannot ratify. Until then, the EU can only have observer status at WIPO.

The WTO and TRIPS

A further dimension to international copyright is given by the WTO and TRIPS. Efficient intellectual property regimes are considered vital to the expansion of world trade. In 1994 the World Trade Organization came into being together with an annex to this agreement called TRIPS – the Trade-Related Aspects of Intellectual Property Rights. The purpose of TRIPS was 'to reduce distortions and impediments to international trade and . . . to ensure that measures and procedures to Intellectual Property rights do not themselves become barriers to legitimate trade'. The threat of trade sanctions has meant that there has been a greater incentive for countries to sign up to TRIPS, adopt stronger copyright laws to combat piracy and to enforce protection. In 1995 WTO and WIPO made an agreement to co-operate. TRIPS signatories were obliged to comply with the main articles of the Berne and Rome conventions.

All developed nations have signed TRIPS. Developing nation members were obliged to implement its provisions by 1 January 2000, and the deadline for the WTO least-developed countries is 1 January 2006. Many of the new rights contained in TRIPS, such as protection for computer programs, compilations of data, and rental right, were incorporated into the WIPO Copyright and the WIPO Performers and Phonograms treaties.

European Union harmonization

Following the publication of a Green Paper in 1988, the Commission of the

European Communities embarked on a programme to harmonize the various copyright laws of member states. The areas where harmonization was seen to be necessary were: computer programs, the term of protection, rental and lending and certain neighbouring rights, databases, private copying, satellite and cable broadcasting, and moral rights. The following is a selection of those relevant to the library and information profession which have been implemented into the UK Act. As it has been the most controversial directive and is the subject of the most recent changes to the Act of 1988, the Copyright Directive is discussed at greater length than the others.

Computer programs

The law relating to computer programs was the subject of the first amendment to the Act. It was amended by the Copyright (Computer Programs) Regulations 1992 (SI 1992 No. 3233) to comply with EU Directive No. 91/250/EEC on Computer Software. Computer programs are protected as literary works, which gives them the full protection of the Berne Convention. The UK already protected computer programs in the 1988 Act, but the Directive allowed certain exceptions which were absent from the 1988 Act, such as the ability to make a back-up copy where necessary.

Term of protection

EC Directive 93/98/EEC on the Duration of Copyright directed member states to extend the term of protection for copyright literary, dramatic, musical and artistic works and films from 50 to 70 years after the year of death of the author. This became law in the UK on 1 January 1996 with the Duration of Copyright and Rights in Performances Regulations (SI 1995 No. 3297).

Rental and lending

Public lending was separated from commercial rental with the Copyright and Related Rights Regulations 1996 (SI 1996 No. 2967) which implemented the European Council Directive on Rental and Lending (92/100/EEC). This directive established that libraries had to be licensed to lend copyright-protected material to the public, as well as for rental on a commercial basis. Lending was defined as making a copy of a work available for use on terms that it will or may be returned, otherwise than for a direct or indirect or commercial advantage through an establishment which is accessible to the public. Public libraries were obviously subject to the new rules. (See Chapter 3.)

Databases

After discussions spanning four years the controversial European Council Directive on the legal protection of databases (96/9/EC) was adopted and was implemented into UK law by the Copyright and Rights in Database Regulations (SI 1997 No. 3032). The Directive introduced the new form of intellectual property protection for databases to prevent unfair extraction and reutilization of their contents. This law also changed the exception for fair dealing for research and private study to fair dealing for non-commercial research or private study when copying from a copyright-protected database. This was the first attack on fair dealing. The next attack came with the Copyright Directive.

The Copyright Directive

Arguably the most controversial directive to come from Brussels was the Copyright Directive: the European Council Directive on the harmonization of certain aspects of Copyright and Related Rights in the Information Society (2001/29/EC). This was the directive which proposed to harmonize the definition of the reproduction right and the exceptions and limitations (the so-called private copying), and introduced the new rights which the EU has to implement in order to ratify the WIPO treaties of 1996 (see above). The text of this directive was first seen in 1997 and it was not adopted until June 2001. The controversy continued with implementation. Member states were obliged to implement the provisions of the Copyright Directive within eighteen months from date of adoption, i.e. December 2002, rather than two years. However, as so often happens, the timetable slipped and implementation did not take place until more than two years from date of adoption (in the UK, 31 October 2003). Consequently the UK, along with most of the other member states, was taken to task by the EU. Only two member states, Greece and Denmark, implemented the Directive on time.

The UK government body responsible for copyright, the Patent Office, held a consultation between August and October 2002 which produced over 300 responses from rights holders and users criticizing the original proposed text.

Process and progress of directives

In order to understand why EC Directives take so long to be implemented it is important that the process is understood. Proposals for directives are generated by EC officials in Brussels, discussed with national representatives, sent out as drafts for comment to selected organizations (usually with tight deadlines), reviewed at hearings for invited representatives of all parties concerned, debated by a Council of Ministers working group, agreed by the Council of Permanent

Representatives (COREPER), redrafted as necessary and then submitted to the European Parliament and Council within three to six months for adoption as directives. Member states usually have two years in which to implement provisions into national law if they are not to break European Commission rules. The process is even more complicated as the European Parliament can suggest further amendments which result in further drafts sent out for discussion and comment. Depending on the controversial nature of the directive, the governments of member states, officials in Brussels and MEPs are lobbied furiously by interested parties with much to gain or lose by a simple change in a clause. Controversial directives usually end with a compromise, as happened with the Database Directive.

Different legal traditions and practices in Europe

Another important delaying factor is caused by the differences between the legal traditions of UK/Ireland and mainland Europe. With respect to copyright, those countries on the European mainland follow civil law, whereas the UK and the Republic of Ireland along with other English-speaking nations (USA, Australia, South Africa, etc.) follow common law. Under civil law, authors have an inalienable right to their intellectual property. In other words, it is part of their civil rights. Under common law, copyright is not an absolute right. It is granted only by law. This is an important distinction and explains why harmonization of copyright across EU member states can be so difficult.

Generally speaking, citizens of the civil law countries do not understand how common law countries function with regard to abiding by copyright laws, and vice versa. Fair dealing and the American fair use are examples of these differences in understanding. The civil law countries fail to see why common law countries are so protective of the concept of fair dealing. The civil law countries appear to allow more substantial copying (even whole works) under exceptions for 'private copying'. To compensate authors and other rights holders in mainland Europe (apart from Italy) payments obtained from levies on copying material such as tapes, CDs and photocopiers are collected and distributed. In some member states this is administered by government. The UK Government has resisted pressure from Europe to incorporate such levies as they are seen to be an additional burden on consumers and as a tax, as authors and rights holders are not compensated directly for copying of their works. Instead, the UK Government prefers to provide limited exceptions and encourage licensing solutions, as these are seen to be fairer to both authors and consumers.

Controversial issues in the Directive

The EU list of exceptions was a closed one, meaning that only those exceptions listed could be implemented in the national laws of member states. Only one exception was mandatory: temporary (transient or incidental reproductions, e.g. caching, could be defined as non-infringing. The rest of the exceptions were optional, so member states could pick from the 'shopping list' what they wanted to include in their laws. Some would choose all; some may not choose any, etc. Many of the articles were accompanied by a condition that the rights holder was compensated. Unnecessary distinctions were being made between analogue and digital, and print and electronic.

It was clear that the EU did not like the fact that much 'private copying' existed (despite levies) and tried to make sure that copying other than for non-commercial purposes was banned under any research, education or library and archive exception. This was a major concern to information professionals as the realization dawned that changes would have to be made to fair dealing and library copying for research. The Patent Office representatives confirmed early in the process that there would be no copying for commercial research allowed following implementation into UK law. The officials admitted that they were not in favour of having to make these changes and appreciated that they would cause problems with compliance, especially for those in industry and commerce. They admitted that they frequently argued against the restrictions at meetings of the Council of Ministers working group, but were always outvoted. There was no option but to implement the terms of the Directive.

Technical protection systems and lawful copying

The other major concern for information professionals was the article concerning the protection for technical devices against unlawful circumvention. This was one of the WIPO obligations, and deliberations to agree the appropriate terminology took a very long time because of the controversy. In a nutshell, the Copyright Directive states that if a technical protection device or system is employed to prevent access or copying, then this may not be circumvented for unlawful purposes. For example, if a website prevents unauthorized access to the contents by some technical means, then it will be unlawful to interfere in order to circumvent such protection to gain access. Normally, authorization to access such contents, e.g. an e-journal, is by subscription contract anyway. If, however, access is open to anyone and a person wishes to make a copy for a *lawful* purpose – under a statutory exception, e.g. for research, for Parliamentary or judicial proceedings or for another person with a visual impairment, etc. – how can a copy be taken if a technical measure blocks any copying? It may not be circumvented as that would be unlawful, so what happens in such cases? If no circumvention is allowed, permission (and probably payment) would have to be obtained first in order to access and use the protected work. This would effectively nullify any statutory permissions. The whole point of a statutory *permission* is that no further authorization is required.

Consumer groups (librarians and information professionals, and education, research and disability groups) were extremely concerned and raised these concerns many times in Brussels during the adoption process. The outcome was a compromise to the effect that safeguards may be included in national legislation to enable a beneficiary of an exception to benefit. Governments are allowed to intervene if there is no satisfactory voluntary agreement reached between rights holders and consumers, to ensure that the exception can be carried out. However, there was a sting in the tail in that if there is a contract or licence to use the work then governments will be prevented from intervening. The UK solution to these safeguards is given in Chapter 7, pages 127–8.

Communication to the public

Trying to keep both users and rights holders happy with the drafting of the technical protection systems safeguards severely delayed the implementation process. However, another major delay was caused by the definition of 'communication to the public'. In the draft consultation document, the Patent Office proposed to define this to include the broadcasting right and the making-available right. Broadcasting was seen to be one-way communication to the public, whereas *making available* to the public was interactive. It was important that the language of the definition was watertight. Many rights holders were concerned with the original draft definition. Users, too, were unhappy about the several definitions of *making available* in the Act which appeared to be contradictory.

Beyond Europe

The European Union is not working in isolation. The copyright laws in most other countries have all had to catch up with international IP obligations of TRIPS and Berne and/or the WIPO treaties. Some of the more remarkable laws have been included below.

USA

The current copyright law in the USA dates from 1976. Like the UK Act it has been amended several times to take account of international agreements and changes in technology. Not surprisingly, the legislation in the USA is as controversial as that of Europe. US and EU officials were the ones who drafted the original WIPO proposals which were seen to be very unbalanced in favour of rights holders.

Digital Millennium Copyright Act

The Digital Millennium Copyright Act (DMCA) 1998 implemented the provisions contained in the WIPO copyright treaties, including the right to legal protection for technical protection systems. The main issue for librarians was how to preserve the principle of *fair use*. Whereas the UK has the defence of fair dealing for limited access to copyright-protected works for specific purposes, the USA has *fair use* which is different in that specific uses are not outlined. The argument for fair use access was similar to that in the UK and Europe: if access to works is protected by technological measures, how can the public exercise fair use with regard to those works? As a result of heavy lobbying, libraries and non-profit educational institutions were given a very limited 'browsing right' to circumvent a technical protection measure in order to review a work before purchasing or licensing. However, once the review was completed, the work could not be accessed again. The question still remained unanswered about how a library could obtain the means to circumvent the technical measure, if the librarian is unable to purchase any equipment in order to circumvent, as the selling of equipment is prohibited under the ban on infringing devices. This was also a question raised in Europe. Unlike the UK, there are no specific safeguards proposed, but Congress agreed to review any adverse effects of the legislation after a specified time.

Another controversial and worrying issue for US information professionals was that online service providers (OSPs), including libraries and educational institutions, could be liable for copyright infringement if they allowed, wittingly or unwittingly, the trafficking of infringing works. After lobbying, this was subject to a limitation but only if a service provider registered as such and could comply with the restrictions. Libraries and educational institutions offering online services would have to be careful to ensure copyright compliance. There are also data-privacy and the right-to-read implications. OSPs have already been subpoenaed under the DMCA to release names of alleged violators of the Act.

One positive inclusion in the DMCA was that US librarians were given an extension to their version of the library regulations (Section 108) to allow preservation of works in digital format.

Sonny Bono Copyright Term Extension Act

In 1998 the Sonny Bono Copyright Term Extension was enacted to extend the term of protection. This act added 20 years to terms of protection, giving individual authors protection for life plus 70 years, bringing personal authors in the USA in line with Europe.

It also gave corporate authors protection for 95 years. Works created by corporate authors, such as Disney and the New York Times, originally received protection for 75 years from the date of their creation, and the Act now gave them an additional 20 years of exploitation. This was seen as very controversial. It came about as a result of intense lobbying by a group of powerful corporate copyright holders, most visibly Disney, which wanted to protect their characters for as long as possible. The legislation was familiarly called the Mickey Mouse Protection Act.

In October 2001 a challenge was made to the Sonny Bono Act by Eric Eldred and supported by concerned groups including the American Library Association and other libraries, and in February 2002 the American Supreme Court agreed to debate whether or not this law was constitutional. Those against the extension argued that it did nothing to encourage creativity because the longer term blocked public domain use. However, in January 2003 the Supreme Court ruled in a 7–2 decision in favour of Disney and copyright owners. The library community, however, did win a hard-fought battle to be able to use works in the last 20 years of protection for purposes of preservation, scholarship or research, as long as the work is not subject to normal commercial exploitation or is not available at a reasonable price.

UCITA

Another controversial law is the Uniform Computer Information Transactions Act (UCITA). This is a proposed state contract law designed to standardize the law and provide the default rules for licensing software and all other forms of digital information. UCITA is applicable to information in electronic form: computer software, online databases, electronic journals, e-books, CD-ROMs and videos. In brief, UCITA validates any non-negotiated contracts to use these materials such as shrink-wrap and click-use licences. So far it has become law in only two states, and American librarians are hoping that it will fail to become universal.

TEACH

In October 2002 the US Congress passed the Technology, Education and Copyright Harmonization (TEACH) Act. This came into being because of a lobby of librarians and educators during the run-up to the DMCA. It concerns the use of copyright-protected materials in distance education. Subject to certain restrictions, the act gives permission for educators to use certain copyrighted works without permission or payment of royalties to rights holders.

In the pipeline

New legislation called the Digital Choice and Freedom Act was introduced in Congress in 2002 which, if enacted, would allow consumers to copy legally CDs, DVDs and other digital works for their personal use.

The US still has no protection for non-original databases. This is likely in the near future, although it still has not been introduced into Congress.

Australia

Australian copyright legislation is based on the UK Act but without the EU harmonization changes.

The Copyright Amendment (Digital Agenda) Act

Australia's legislation to implement the WIPO treaties was the Copyright Amendment (Digital Agenda) Act 2000. Compared with the EU and US legislation, which favours rights holders over users, it is seen to be extremely well balanced, mainly because of the successful campaigning by the Australian Libraries Copyright Committee (ALCC) and the Australian Digital Alliance (ADA). This can be illustrated by describing their fair dealing exception. The Digital Agenda Act does not extend the scope of fair dealing but neither does it narrow it down as has happened in the UK. When making a fair dealing copy for research and study – note, neither research nor study is qualified – users have to take into account the commercial availability of the material and the effect of its intended use on the market. However, if only 10% or less of the work is copied, the other factors do not have to be considered. Fair dealing applies to online and digital as well as print-based uses. Also in Australia, it is not an infringement for libraries, archives, museums and galleries to make digital copies of material in their collections for preservation and internal management purposes, and to make such copies available on intranets for staff use, subject to certain safeguards. Another difference between the UK and Australia is that the Australian legislation makes collective licensing in educational establishments statutory, and the Digital Agenda Act has extended these licences to the online environment. Regarding the WIPO provision to prevent circumvention of technical protection systems right, Australia has introduced a limited set of exceptions for permitted purposes to resolve the problem of legitimate access to works protected by such systems.

Contracts and copyright

There has also been some groundbreaking research in Australia into the issue of contract over-riding copyright. The Copyright Law Review Committee, a specialist advisory body established in 1983 to inquire into and report to government on specific copyright law issues, published a report in 2002 on contract versus copyright law. Called *Contract and Copyright*, the report has been hailed as one of the first detailed reviews of the relationship between copyright and contract in the world. The report concluded that contract law should *not* override copyright law. The Committee said that it was 'most concerned that, in practice, there are very considerable disincentives to users ever seeking to defend their rights while there are very powerful incentives for copyright owners to seek to enforce what might otherwise be objectionable terms'. The report goes on to say that: 'it is impractical to expect copyright users to assume the risk of expensive litigation to maintain the copyright exceptions where individual contracts purport to exclude or modify them'. The Committee recommended that Australian copyright law be amended so that agreements or provisions of agreements that exclude or modify the exceptions in the Act, e.g. shrink-wrap or click-use non-negotiated agreements, have no effect. The report is at present with the Australian Government for consideration.

South Africa

South Africa has been described as a third-world country masquerading as a first-world country. Although many international organizations such as WIPO and the United Nations recognize South Africa as a country still in development, under TRIPS it is considered as developed because it has been a signatory to Berne since 1928. While its neighbouring countries are still considered developing and can take advantage of benefits from this status, e.g. TRIPS, South Africa cannot. Its laws are that of the developed world but its practices are that of a developing country.

South Africa and its neighbours formed the Southern African Development Community (SADC). Members are Angola, Botswana, Democratic Republic of the Congo, Lesotho, Malawi, Mauritius, Mozambique, Namibia, Seychelles, South Africa, Swaziland, Tanzania, Zambia and Zimbabwe. While these countries have harmonization of their laws regarding industrial property, there are no co-operative copyright treaties among the SADC countries, nor is there any harmonization of copyright laws in the Southern African region. All SADC countries except Mozambique have some form of copyright protection and legislation. Most copyright laws in Africa, including South Africa, are based on the 1911 UK Act. Most of them are very outdated. South Africa's legislation is the most up to date. As a result, the importance, application and interpretation of copyright principles in this region differ from one member country to the next.

Copyright Act 1978

The main South African copyright legislation is the Copyright Act No. 98 of 1978 which has been amended several times. The latest amendment (2002) applied to broadcasts and collection societies, mainly with respect to compliance with some of the requirements of the WIPO treaties of 1996. South Africa is a signatory to the WIPO treaties of 1996 but does not yet have the appropriate amending legislation in place so cannot accede until then. There is also a set of Regulations that relate to allowing the copying of handouts for classroom purposes, as well as copying by librarians and archivists. The Act contains similar exceptions to the Copyright, Designs and Patents Act 1988 before it was amended by EU harmonization. The copyright term for literary, dramatic, musical and artistic works is the Berne minimum of life plus 50 years.

The need for adequate exceptions

Since 1999 the education sector has presented a number of copyright position papers, and has made various recommendations to the South African Government with regard to issues affecting education, e.g. electronic copyright, and provisions for disabled people, the distance learner and the illiterate, with the hope of amending the copyright legislation to give appropriate exceptions. This has not yet happened. There were two sets of proposals by the Government to amend the Regulations (in 1988) and the Act (2000), but as these were very restrictive to education, they were withdrawn after strong objections from the education sector.

'The strict copyright rules make access to information very difficult and in order to obtain current information, very often the only choice is to copy, whether legally or illegally. In rural areas where most people are illiterate or poorly educated, they do not have the resources to pay for food and basic amenities, let alone books and copyright fees' (D. Nicholson, Chapter 10, page 171). Adequate exceptions are needed for South Africa in line with those of the other developing countries in the region. In 2001 the education sector began discussions on these issues with the Publishing Association of South Africa (PASA), as well as with the International Publishing Association (IPA). These were, unfortunately, not successful because of the major differences of opinion regarding fair use and multiple copying for non-profit educational purposes. The education sector, including libraries, is continuing its campaign by lobbying the South African Government, which it is hoped will lead to eventual amendment and updating of the copyright legislation.

Ten things to remember from this chapter

▪ the first copyright law was the Statute of Anne in 1710

▪ copyright laws in the UK (and in many other nations) are mainly based on trading agreements

▪ most copyright laws in the world are based on the Berne Convention

▪ the three-step test comes from the Berne Convention

▪ the © comes from the Universal Copyright Convention

▪ the World Intellectual Property Organization (WIPO) is responsible for the major copyright conventions

▪ TRIPS obliges all nations to sign up to and comply with the Berne and Rome principles

▪ the Copyright, Designs and Patents Act 1988 has been amended many times because of the single market initiative to harmonize copyright laws of EU member states

▪ the WIPO Treaties' obligation to apply legal protection to technical protection systems conflicts with statutory copying permissions and has caused problems in Europe, the USA and Australia

▪ compliance with international copyright agreements imposed because of trade distortions often conflicts with developing nations' educational and literacy needs.

9 Case studies and frequently asked questions

Hopefully many of the questions information professionals have about copyright have already been answered in this guide. Having grasped the basics and using a modicum of common sense, readers should be able to work many of the problems out by themselves. But there will *always* be further questions about copyright! However experienced or knowledgeable an information professional becomes, they will still need reassurance on copyright issues and so there will be more questions. This chapter contains a small sample of some of the more complex issues.

Prescribed library or not?

Q Is my library prescribed? I work for a children's charity.

A The types of library considered to be prescribed and able to take advantage of the library regulations are given in Chapter 2, page 20 and Figure 2.1. I presume the charity is not run for profit, so you pass the main hurdle. It is likely that your library fits into the description of 'any library which encourages the study of bibliography, education, fine arts, history, languages, law, literature, medicine, music, philosophy, religion, science (including natural and social science) or technology'. Libraries of any type encourage study, so I am sure your charity is covered by this definition in one way or another. Yes, your library will be 'prescribed'.

Commercial research or not?

Q I work for a non-departmental public body. Research undertaken is funded mainly by government or research council money, but an increasing amount of research is being funded by commercial organizations. The library also allows researchers from other academic and commercial organizations to use the service. We currently charge commercial visitors the cost of photocopying only when carrying out their own copying from the library stock. We also supply requested documents by post under the library regulations. What is the situation following the Copyright Directive changes?

A Fair dealing for commercial research is no longer permitted, so if your commercial users are copying for research for a commercial purpose then this becomes illegal unless specifically authorized by licence or with permission.

Similarly the library is no longer allowed to supply items to users (under the library regulations) if they are needed for research for a commercial purpose. So, if you wish to carry on giving this service, you will need to obtain a licence from the CLA to cover this practice. See Chapter 6 for the various licensing solutions available. With regard to the question of funding, this question has been raised within educational circles where the research is often funded by external companies. However, the Patent Office has assured information professionals that if the main purpose of the research is educational then how funding is obtained is immaterial. This may be the case here as well, as you are not set up for profit.

Current awareness

Q I work in a law library which has a CLA licence. We circulate current awareness bulletins throughout the firm including offices overseas. Our Singapore office wishes to send the bulletin out to clients and wants us to supply these clients with articles quoted in the bulletin. The bulletin contains abstracts of articles written by employees and also from external publications. We do not abstract more than one article from a single issue of a journal in each bulletin. Is what we are doing OK?

A First of all, there appears to be no problem with the bulletin itself as the abstracts are written in-house or obtained from the journals. Therefore, it is fine to send the bulletin to Singapore as it does not contain any copyright material belonging to others (apart from abstracts that accompany articles in journals, which is allowed in the Act). I presume your licence allows the circulation of articles within the organization to authorized users within the firm. However, you need to check whether this covers sending to clients, especially clients of your offices overseas. If not, then you may not supply them. They will have to make their own arrangements to receive them.

Electronic signatures

Q Our library is about to move over to an electronic interlibrary loans package. On this new system users can submit their loan requests electronically. We would like to know if it is still necessary for users to fill in a paper copy of their request containing their signature? Would it be breaching copyright legislation if we didn't have copies of the paper requests, or does an electronic signature now suffice?

A This is difficult to answer since the change in the law which accepts the validity of an electronic signature is rather complex and we have to interpret it as best we can. See Chapter 2, page 23 for details. Government officials have stated that they believe that any form of signature which clearly identifies an individual and is not easily used by others is likely to be acceptable. It is really a matter of whether you think that the electronic signature is enough to satisfy the requirement for it to be an authenticated personal signature: 'uniquely linked to and capable of identifying the signatory'.

Reading onto tapes

Q   I work in a public library and am currently working on a reader development project in which I have set up 'reading groups' in day-care centres for older people. These activities have been discussion and reminiscence sessions based around readings and poems which I have selected on particular themes, such as childhood, schooldays, wartime, holidays, etc. These have been very successful and people's responses to the readings, and particularly the memories these have prompted, have been very interesting and worthwhile. We are now working on producing a tape to include some of the readings and poems used in those sessions, along with the memories and stories they have evoked among the people in the groups. We have been recording people's memories and comments, and are now at the stage where we want to record the readings, etc., hence the need to look into where we stand regarding copyright issues. The extracts we want to include are typically two pages from in-copyright novels, biographies and poems which evoke the past and so hopefully bring back memories for the listeners, as well as promoting an interest in the books and in reading generally. Obviously we would include acknowledgements of the authors and publishers of the works used. We plan to produce several copies of each tape. At least half of these will go into libraries for people to borrow free of charge. Copies will also be given to the day centres which have taken part in the project. Tapes will also be included in the resource packs I'm producing of pre-selected books and poems for staff to run further reading-based activities themselves. Other copies will be used as evidence of the work of this project and given to interested parties to promote awareness of this reader development work. Our intention is not to sell them or make any money out of them. The main aim is to share the pleasure of reading and show the people who have taken part that their memories and views are valued.

A   The rights issues appear complicated but may not necessarily be so. To begin with, it is important to ask questions about whether the proposal is likely to be covered by a statutory exception, whether the works are being exploited and whether the legitimate interests of the authors are being unreasonably prejudiced.

Reading reasonable extracts from copyright-protected works in public is not seen as infringing copyright (s. 59) so no problem there. The Act goes on to state that: 'Copyright in a work is not infringed by the making of a sound recording . . . of a reading or recitation which . . . does not infringe copyright in the work, provided that the recording . . . consists mainly of material in relation to which it is not necessary to rely on that [permission]'. This means, I think, that a recording may be made of the reading as long as most of the rest of the recording consists of material which has been authorized for copying in some way, i.e. where permission has been obtained, the copying is licensed or the material is in the public domain. One could say also that recording these extracts onto tape could be covered by fair dealing for the purposes of criticism or review (s. 30 (1)), and this assumes that multiple copies may be made for publication. However, as this is a large project, it might be safer to ask permission from publishers – and because this is a non-commercial venture, permission should be forthcoming. Recording comments by the older people needs to be cleared at the time, as there is copyright in their performances, and it is assumed this will not pose a problem either. At the same time, it makes sense also to obtain clearance for any other potential uses, whether planned or unforeseen. You never know, at a later date some other librarian may want to put them on a public network or a broadcasting company may want to use them. If they have been cleared to begin with, it makes it a lot easier later on. As you are not selling the recordings, you are not profiting from them so it could not be said that you were unreasonably prejudicing the legitimate interests of the authors. If you did decide to sell them then it might be necessary to clear each extract with the publishers/authors depending on whether you were recovering costs and/or making a profit.

Making compilations from ERA recordings

Q We have an ERA licence and provide an off-air recording service to the whole university, mainly on the subjects of art, media and culture. This collection includes many feature films. The university also holds courses in film production. A video technician does the recording and the tapes follow the ERA conditions of labelling. No facility is provided for student copying but we do lend the videos for a week (mainly because we have many part-time students who attend only once a week). In the past students have made compilations of extracts from different programmes (not just films) that they have used for presentation purposes to student colleagues and academic staff in a classroom situation. The compilations are an important part of their course. Should we allow students to continue to do this? Currently they make these copies while the video is on loan to them, and we cannot know what they are going to do with the resulting tape. If not, what are the practical alternatives? Since we use 3M Kwik cases to secure the videos, we always loan the video even if it is just going to be watched in the library. This means that we cannot prevent them leaving the building, once loaned and removed from the case. Should we be asking all borrowers to sign something when they borrow a tape to say they abide by the ERA licence or each time they take one out?

A The ERA licence allows you to make the recordings and make extracts from recordings to be used in digitized courseware packages, as long as access is on the licensee's premises only. So compilations may be made. Recordings may also be loaned to students within limits, but as ERA is concerned about infringing copies being made, it would be safer to restrict copying to campus only in order to control the making of such extracts. Students should, therefore, sign a statement to this effect. However, that said, section 32 (2) allows an educational establishment, running courses on the making of films or film soundtracks, to make copies from sound recordings, films and broadcasts in the course of, or in preparation for, instruction in the making of films or film soundtracks, provided the copying is done by the person giving or receiving instruction, it is acknowledged and it is for a non-commercial purpose. So students may copy for this purpose. No mention is made here of on-site or off-site copying.

Downloading music

Q Is it advisable for our library users to be able to listen to music downloaded from the internet? Should we allow the public to download the music to take away?

A Listening to music without making a permanent copy is likely to be acceptable as long as the music is from legitimate websites offering such services. There could be payments involved and/or restrictions to make sure that copies are not kept too long on the server cache.

Since the concern by the music industry over the last few years about downloading and file sharing (see case law in Chapter 7, pages 136–7), downloading to take away without payment would definitely not be seen to be fair and would need authorization from rights holders. Therefore, any music downloaded from legitimate websites will probably be subject to payment and restrictions. Such payments would have to be built into your service. There is the possibility of co-operation between public libraries and the music industry to make this a bona fide licensed activity of benefit to both parties. This is something which LACA has raised with the BPI in the long term.

Previewing videos and DVDs in a public library

Q   Is it permissible to offer a 'pay per view' facility in a public library, to pre-view a DVD and/or video? This would be to give the customer an opportu-nity to preview the material before borrowing. If it is possible, would the viewing equipment have to be in a separate room/screened-off area, where no other customer could see it, or could it be situated in an open-plan pub-lic area? Would there be a restriction of how much of a particular DVD or video could be watched like this, or for a particular length of time?

A   The videos are loaned for domestic play only, not for public performance. Viewing a video in the library (as a public place) would therefore infringe copyright in the performance. There is no exception which covers this. Having a separate room for previewing purposes would not solve the prob-lem because it would still be within a public building, and even if only one person is watching a video at a time it would still be a public viewing because any members of the public could avail themselves of the service. There are safer ways of previewing, such as reading a review.

Copyright term of manuscripts

Q   My library holds some original manuscripts of works which have subse-quently been published. Are these manuscripts subject to the published copyright term of life plus 70 years or do they have unpublished status until (2039) at least? The reason for the question is my library may want to dig-itize these originals and put selections of the digitized facsimiles on the web.

A   The copyright term of a work depends on the life of the author. If the author died over 70 years ago then the work is out of copyright. It is the same for published or unpublished works except that works which were never pub-lished before the current Act became law in 1989 are still protected until at least 2039. However, if during this time a work was published, then the standard term of life plus 70 years kicks in. In this case, the manuscript sta-tus of the works no longer counts. To give an example, if an author died in 1900, any of his published works would clearly be out of copyright but any unpublished works would still be in copyright until 2039. If one of the unpublished works were to have been published, say in 2000, it would not have any copyright protection (although the publisher would have the 25-year publication term).

So, as your manuscripts have been published, the term runs from the end of the year of the death of the author plus 70 years. The manuscripts or extracts from those out of copyright may therefore be communicated to the public on the web. If, on the other hand, these works had never been published, then despite the fact that the author is long dead, the work would still be in copyright. The decision then would be more difficult as the Act allows no exceptions for this. It is likely, however, that risks would be low.

Networking local studies material

Q   Our library authority has been given some funding to digitize and network a collection of local studies material, some of which is old and probably out of copyright and some which may still be in copyright. The collection includes photographs, maps, letters and some publications and leaflets. What steps should we take and where do we start?

A   The first step is to make a decision about what content to include and how much time you have to spend on clearance. To play safe, material which is clearly out of copyright could be included first. However, there will be many works in the collection still in copyright which may be considered ideal for inclusion on a network at a future date. Digitizing and making such works available on the network is likely to involve a lot more work in tracking copyright owners and in clearance.

The next step is to establish the copyright status of all the works and whether they have ever been published. This may not be easy but nevertheless attempts must be made. Those works which are out of copyright are considered to be in the public domain and may be safely digitized. Those that are still in copyright will have to be cleared with rights holders. Note that although your library may be the sole owner of the physical work, it may not necessarily own the rights in the work. However, when a work was acquired by your library, permission may have been given to copy and use. If not, then some detective work is called for.

If tracing rights becomes impossible, consider whether it is worth taking the risk in digitizing the work and making it available on the network. The law says, however, that if after making a reasonable attempt to trace the rights holders it can be assumed that the work is out of copyright *or* the author or authors have been dead for 70 years or more, then copying may take place. If one cannot make this assumption, then, depending on the risks, one should consider making a disclaimer as well as putting some money aside against the copyright owner appearing. With really old works, especially unpublished photographs, where there are no traces to follow, the risk of copyright infringement is probably very low. Even if a photographer did turn up to claim the work, this would have to be proved, for example, by showing that he/she is in possession of the negative of the photograph in question. Where possible, acknowledgement of the author should *always* be given.

With the more current material, one of the major problems will be to overcome the resistance of rights holders, usually publishers, to allow their works to be digitized and made available on a network. They will have to be convinced that their works will not be abused or misused and that they will not lose out financially. An author or a publisher will be reluctant to give carte blanche permission for a work to be electronically available without some guarantee that it will not be misused or made available on a network where they fear that it could be accessed by individuals in countries with inadequate copyright protection. Another concern is the potential for violation of an author's moral rights. Works can be manipulated easily while in electronic format, which infringes the author's right of integrity and increases the risk of plagiarism. Rights holders may therefore demand some sort of security.

Where possible, involve legal advisers when negotiating licences and permissions, especially for the more current material. The terms and conditions set by rights holders in a contract or licence must be understood. If your library fails to operate within the terms of the licence then the library as party to the contract will be liable. Therefore, any terms which are going to be difficult to adhere to will need to be considered very carefully. Terms and conditions are as important as the price.

There will be rights in the network as a database. These rights will belong to the database maker. It is advisable to establish who will have access to works included on the network and for what purposes. This will depend to a large extent on any contractual obligations which may have been negotiated, but it should also be driven by the policy of your organization.

Careful consideration will need to be given to network management if it is necessary to convince rights holders that the library will not be encouraging or condoning infringing acts. For example, if remote access by users is to be given to the works, then how will this be controlled? Will access be blocked by a technological device? Will users have to be registered and obtain access via a password? Will they have to read and accept terms of use before accessing works? How will this be monitored?

Clearly, those who work in the for-profit sector may need to access the network at some time, either on-site in the library or remotely. If your library (having the rights in the network) decides that only non-commercial copying by users may take place, careful consideration will have to be given on how to stick to such a policy. Also, if contracts with rights holders forbid such copying, how will this be adhered to and what will be the risks of non-compliance? There may not be an easy way to distinguish between commercial and non-commercial uses in any case. Not all copying by 'commercial' users is for direct gain.

In the long term, your library may decide to be involved in generating income by trading its information for commercial gain. In this case, all the rights in the content should be cleared for this purpose. If necessary, consideration should be given to methods of passing royalties on to rights holders for uses of their works.

10 Learning more about copyright

In this chapter you will learn about:

- the committees and bodies that lobby on copyright on behalf of the profession
- websites giving information on intellectual property
- the relevant copyright statutory material
- references and other resources on copyright
- training courses.

This chapter is for those who wish to explore behind the scenes to learn more about copyright. Who lobbies on behalf of information professionals? Where can I go for further information or if I have a question? How can I keep up to date on copyright and licensing, and so on?

Working for the profession: lobbying activities

There are many supporters of strong intellectual property rights today. Publishers, licensing organizations, media companies and their trade associations view ever-increased rights for copyright owners as the best way to maximize their potential revenue. It is somewhat harder, however, to find equally prominent defenders of the other half of the copyright balance, namely the needs of the public to have reasonable legitimate access to copyright material. This can be attributed in some degree to the fact that many advocates of stronger rights have a financial interest in such an outcome. The wider public interest in being able to access to this material is more diffuse and usually has no direct economic motive, and so so is less likely to attract professional advocates. The library, information and archive sector, however, is proud to view itself as a custodian of the public interest in this regard. Described below are the national and international organizations representing the library, archive, education and museum sectors, as well as the public interest on copyright matters.

LACA

The Libraries and Archives Copyright Alliance is an alliance of major professional organizations in the librarianship, archivist and information science professions, together with organizations representing visually impaired and educational users of copyright materials. LACA is the main UK voice speaking and lobbying on all aspects of copyright and related rights on behalf of UK libraries, archives and information services and their users. The member organizations currently represented on LACA are: ARLIS, Aslib, BIALL, the British Library, CILIP (representing all sectors), ECUF, IAML (UK), the RNIB, the Society of Archivists, the Society of Chief Librarians in England and Wales, and SCONUL. There are also several independent copyright experts in the group.

LACA, which represents the unified voice of the information profession on copyright, meets three times a year to discuss issues surrounding copyright and licensing. Its basic concern is that the economic rights of creators and information providers are balanced with the needs of library and information staff and their users to gain access to information. LACA responds to all relevant government and European Union consultation documents and draft directives on copyright and related rights, and works closely with EBLIDA. It sets up frequent meetings with the Government to discuss issues of concern. It liaises with collecting societies and rights holder representatives on licensing issues. The LACA web pages, accessed via the CILIP website, contain recent responses and topics of concern.

CILIP

The Chartered Institute of Library and Information Professionals is the cornerstone of LACA, as it convenes the alliance. CILIP's copyright adviser, who is also the Secretary of LACA, provides telephone, e-mail and written advice to CILIP members on copyright and related rights. CILIP is represented on the EBLIDA Copyright Experts Group and on IFLA CLM (see below), as well as on various national committees dealing with copyright.

CILIP copyright posters

To mitigate copyright liability, CILIP advises that library and information centres have suitable notices about copyright prominently displayed in areas where copying may take place. These can be created in-house or, if more general posters are required, they can be purchased from CILIP. Two types of copyright poster covering fair dealing for research or private study are available for display next to self-service copying equipment: one for display beside photocopiers and optical scanners, and another, on downloading (whether by digital copying or print output) from databases (portable or otherwise) or the internet, to be displayed next to computers, CD/DVD writers and printers. These are also available in Welsh.

CILIP also sells a poster for display with sound recording loan collections, which those public library services which have signed up to the CILIP (formerly LA)/BPI Agreement are obliged to display next to loan collections of recorded sound material.

Prices and ordering information for all posters can be found on the LACA web pages on the CILIP website.

Museums Copyright Group

This group mainly lobbies on behalf of museums and galleries, and, with a similar agenda to LACA, has forged links with the latter to work together on common issues. Members of LACA attend meetings of the MCG. Its interest is mainly in clearing rights to use materials in collections and obtaining suitable licences. The group has members representing museums, galleries, archives and libraries, including national and regional institutions, and those attached to universities and local authorities.

EFPICC UK

The original European Fair Practices in Copyright Campaign was an alliance of concerned European consumer groups, consumer electronics industries, and education, library and disability groups which formed during the run-up to the adoption of the EU Copyright Directive in order to lobby for sufficient level of access and affordable use of copyrighted information. EBLIDA represented European librarians on EFPICC and was constantly lobbying MEPs. EFPICC disbanded in 2001 but it is still active in the UK, where it meets regularly. Some of the organizations represented include: BUFVC, CILIP, ECUF, Mencap, the NBU, the RNIB, the RNID, SCONUL, the Society of Archivists, and the VLV.

EBLIDA

The European Bureau of Library and Information Documentation Associations describes itself as an independent, non-profit umbrella organization of national library, information, documentation and archive associations in Europe representing the interests of its members to the European institutions, such as the European Commission, European Parliament and the Council of Europe. Subjects on which EBLIDA concentrates are European information society issues, including copyright and licensing, culture and education, and EU enlargement. It promotes unhindered access to information in the digital age, and the role of archives and libraries in achieving this goal.

IFLA

The International Federation of Library Associations and Institutions represents and lobbies for the interests of libraries and information services, as well as the users of such services, worldwide. It has a Committee on Copyright and other Legal Matters (CLM) which meets once a year at the general conference to discuss relevant copyright and other legal issues. IFLA sends delegates to international copyright forums including WIPO and UNESCO. IFLA strongly endorses the notion that notionthat copyright must be balanced. The 'IFLA Position on Copyright in the Digital Environment' states:

> Librarians and information professionals recognize, and are committed to support the needs of their patrons to gain access to copyright works and the information and ideas they contain. They also respect the needs of authors and copyright owners to obtain a fair economic return on their intellectual property. Effective access is essential in achieving copyright's objectives. IFLA supports balanced copyright law that promotes the advancement of society as a whole by giving strong and effective protection for the interests of rights holders as well as reasonable access in order to encourage creativity, innovation, research, education and learning.

IFLA is very concerned that the increased use of licensing and technological protection systems may be distorting the balance toward commercial interests and away from information users. This trend affects information users everywhere, but; it has an even greater effect on those in developing countries who are at a much greater disadvantage.

Details of the work of CLM, including the above statement, press releases and responses to international documents, may be found on the IFLA CLM website (www.ifla.org/III/clm/copy.htm). IFLA also has regular meetings with the International Publishers Association (IPA) to try to resolve some of the more thorny copyright and other issues. CLM is closely allied to another IFLA committee called FAIFE (Freedom of Access to Information and Freedom of Expression). Details of this committee may be found on the IFLA website.

Statutory material on copyright and related issues

The statutory material described below is also published in full text form on the HMSO web pages (www.legislation.hmso.gov.uk). There is still no conformed copy of the Copyright, Designs and Patents Act 1988 available from HMSO so the Act has to be read with all the amending legislation published since 1989. Conformed copies are of course included in the latest editions of well-known legal textbooks on copyright.

Copyright, Designs and Patents Act 1988 (c. 48), London, HMSO. ISBN 0 10 544888 5.
Copyright (Librarians and Archivists) (Copying of Copyright Material) Regulations 1989, SI 1989 No. 1212, HMSO. ISBN 0 11 097212 0.
Copyright (Educational Establishments) (No. 2) Order 1989, SI 1989 No. 1068, HMSO. ISBN 0 11 097068 3.
Copyright (Computer Programs) Regulations 1992, SI 1992 No. 3233, HMSO. ISBN 0 11 025116 4.
Duration of Copyright and Rights in Performances Regulations 1995, SI 1995 No. 3297, HMSO. ISBN 0 11 053833 1.
Copyright and Related Rights Regulations 1996, SI 1996 No. 2967, The Stationery Office Ltd. ISBN 0 11 063334 2.
Copyright and Related Rights Regulations 2003, SI 2003 No. 2498, The Stationery Office Ltd. ISBN 0 11 047709 X.
Copyright and Rights in Databases Regulations 1997, SI 1997 No. 3032, The Stationery Office Ltd. ISBN 0 11 065325 4.
Copyright (Certification of Licensing Scheme for Educational Recording of Broadcasts) (Open University) Order 2003, SI 2003 No. 187, The Stationery Office Ltd. ISBN 0 11 045002 7.
Copyright (Certification of Licensing Scheme for Educational Recording of Broadcasts and Cable Programmes) (Educational Recording Agency Limited) (Amendment) Order 2003, SI 2003 No. 188, The Stationery Office Ltd. ISBN 0 11 045006 X.
Electronic Commerce (EC Directive) Regulations 2002, SI 2002 No. 2013.
Electronic Communications Act 2000, HMSO, ISBN 0 10 540700 3.
Electronic Signatures Regulations 2002, SI 2003 No. 318.

International copyright treaty publications

Publications given below are freely available on websites. For contact details of organizations mentioned see Appendix C.

Universal Copyright Convention, UNESCO, Paris, 1952.
International Convention for the Protection of Performers, Producers of Phonograms and Broadcasting Organisations (Rome Convention), WIPO, 1961.
Berne Convention for the Protection of Literary and Artistic Works, Paris Act 1971, WIPO, Geneva, 1989.
Convention for the Protection of Producers of Phonograms Against Unauthorized Duplication of their Phonograms, WIPO, Geneva, 1971.
TRIPS: Agreement on Trade-Related Aspects of Intellectual Property Rights, WTO, Uruguay, 1994.

WIPO Copyright Treaty, WIPO, Geneva, 1996.
WIPO Performers and Phonograms Treaty, WIPO, Geneva, 1996.

Information on the web

Some other free-access websites providing information and/or news on intellectual property include the following:

- EUROPA *Intellectual Property News* (European Commission),
  http://europa. eu.int/comm/internal_market/en/intprop/news/index.htm.
- the *Copyright Bulletin*, published by UNESCO, provides information on legal developments in the protection of copyright and neighbouring rights at the national and international levels,
  http://unesco.org/culture/copyrightbulletin/.
- *IPR Helpdesk* (a project of the European Commission Enterprise Directorate-General), www.ipr-helpdesk.org/index.htm.
- *The UK Patent Office* website, www.patent.gov.uk.
- news links from the UK Government IP portal,
  www.intellectual-property.gov.uk/news/index.htm.
- *JISC Legal Information Service* provides information on legal issues relevant to IT provision in the UK higher education sector,
  www.jisc.ac.uk/legal/.
- *Managing Information* has current information on copyright issues,
  www.managinginformation.com.
- The *Copyright Management for Scholarship* website, a by-product of the conferences on copyright and universities held in Zwolle in the Netherlands, contains a wide range of information on the topic, and includes links to an extensive range of good practices for each country or region,
  www.surf.nl/copyright/.

Discussion list

Lis-copyseek is an extremely useful discussion group for sharing practical experiences of copyright permission seeking and working within copyright law and licence conditions. This list is available to join mainly by UK HE practitioners and those working in copyright *from the point of view of the users only*. Rights holders and their representatives are not able to apply for membership. Membership requests should be sent to lis-copyseek-request@jiscmail.ac.uk. Contact details and reasons for wishing to join the list should be included.

References and further reading

Archives

Padfield, T. (2004) *Copyright for Archivists and Users of Archives*, 2nd edn, London, Facet Publishing.

Australian copyright

Copyright and Contract (discussed in Chapter 8, page 152), www.law.gov.au/clrc/.

Copyright clearance in the higher education sector

Gadd, E. (2000) Clearing the Way: copyright clearance in UK Libraries, *Library and Information Research News*, **24** (78), 4–12. (This article summarizes and discusses the results of Gadd's copyright clearance research.)

Crown copyright

The Future Management of Crown Copyright, Cm 4300, HMSO, 1999.
HMSO Guidance Notes, www.hmso.gov.uk/guides.htm.
Scottish Guidance Note, www.hmso.gov.uk/guidance/scotgn/scotgn1.htm.
HMSO Class Licence,
    www.clickanduse.hmso.gov.uk/online/cup_online_home.asp.

Deep linking

Eaglesham J. (2001) How Far Does Copyright Extend in Cyberspace?, *Financial Times*, (15 January), 18.
Coombes, S. W. (2001) Deep Linking: an overview, *Copyright World*. Accessed on Field Fisher Waterhouse website, www.ffwlaw.com; Dutch Papers Fail in Internet Copyright Case, *Financial Times*, 23 August 2000, p. 6.

Enforcement

Proposal for a Directive of the European Parliament of the Council on measures and procedures to ensure the enforcement of intellectual property rights (COM (200) 46 final).

General

Cornish, G. P. (2004) *Copyright: interpreting the law for libraries, archives and information services*, 4th edn, London, Facet Publishing.
Cornish, G. P. (2002) *Understanding Copyright in a Week*, 2nd edn, London, Hodder and Stoughton.

Licensing

Giavarra, E. (2001) *Licensing Digital Resources: how to avoid the legal pitfalls*, 2nd edn, EBLIDA, www.eblida.org/ecup/docs/.
A Guide to Licensing Copyright in Schools, www.licensing-copyright.org.
ICOLC statement of licensing principles, www.library.yale.edu/consortia/.
IFLA *Licensing Principles* (2001), www.ifla.org/V/ebpb/copy.htm.

Music

Music Publishers Association (1992). *Code of Fair Practice for Printed Music*, rev. edn, (but due for revision shortly), www.mpaonline.org.uk/code_ofp.html.

South African copyright

Nicholson, D. (2003) *What Has Copyright Got to Do With Newspapers? – an SA perspective*. Paper presented to IFLA Berlin, www.ifla.org/IV/ifla69/papers/059e-Nicholson.pdf.

US copyright

For information on copyright legislation follow the links on the American Library Association website, www.ala.org/.

Visually impaired persons

Copyright & Visual Impairment Joint Industry Guidelines, www.pls.org.uk/publisher/vip_Frontpage.htm.
Copyright (Visually Impaired Persons) Act 2002, The Stationery Office Ltd. ISBN 0 10 543302 0.
Copyright (Visually Impaired Persons) Act 2002 (Commencement) Order 2003, SI 2003 No. 2499, The Stationery Office Ltd. ISBN 0 11 047706 5.

Training courses

A good way of developing professional knowledge about copyright, as well as networking with like-minded colleagues, is to attend a course/workshop/briefing session on copyright. These usually range from half a day to two days depending on complexity. There are often sessions on copyright at professional conferences. Such training sessions are always popular.

Both the information professional organizations, Aslib and CILIP, offer regular training courses on copyright and licensing for information professionals, as do their sectoral special interest groups and branches, but these are more on an ad hoc basis. These may be for beginners or those who want to be updated.

See Appendix C for contact details.

The Copyright Circle, run by Graham Cornish, also offers regular courses on copyright for all sectors, held in various parts of the UK. Paul Pedley, also a consultant, runs copyright courses, mainly for the business sector, for TFPL. See Appendix C for contact details.

Universities and colleges run the occasional course on copyright for their own staff, and some encourage teaching and lecturing staff to attend. The lis-copyseek administrators (see page 169) also run copyright courses from time to time.

Glossary of acronyms and selected terms

ACID	Anti Copying in Design
the Act	Copyright, Designs and Patents Act 1988
ADA	Australian Digital Alliance
ALCC	Australian Libraries Copyright Committee
ALCS	Authors' Licensing and Collecting Society
ARLIS	Art Libraries Society UK and Ireland
article	Any item in an issue of a journal or a periodical, e.g. an article, a letter to the editor, an editorial, an advertisement, or a contents page
Aslib	The Association for Information Management
Berne three-step test	The test for legislators when allowing exceptions in national copyright laws. Reproduction of works is allowed (1) in certain special cases, provided that such reproduction (2) does not conflict with a normal exploitation of the work and (3) does not unreasonably prejudice the legitimate interests of the author
BIALL	British and Irish Association of Law Librarians
BLDSC	British Library Document Supply Centre
BPI	British Phonographic Industry
BSA	Business Software Alliance
BSI	British Standards Institution
BUFVC	British Universities Film and Video Council
CCLI	Christian Copyright Licensing International
CILIP	Chartered Institute of Library and Information Professionals
CLA	Copyright Licensing Agency (owned by the ALCS and PLS)
CLARCS	CLA Rapid Clearance System
CVCP	Committee of Vice-Chancellors and Principals (now called UUK)
DACS	Design and Artists Copyright Society
database	Any structured collection, whether in print or electronic format, of works, data or other material arranged in a systematic or methodical way and individually accessible by electronic or other means
DCMA	Digital Millennium Copyright Act (USA)

dealt with	Sold or let for hire or offered or exposed for sale or let for hire or communicated to the public
declaration form	The prescribed form of words to be signed by an individual before receiving a copy made by a librarian or archivist under the library regulations. There are two forms: one for published works (parts of books and journal articles) and one for unpublished works. Both are shown in Appendices A and B
digitization	The conversion of material into machine-readable form, usually by scanning. This sometimes refers more specifically to conversion into ASCII characters
DRMS	Digital Rights Management Systems
EBLIDA	European Bureau of Library, Information and Documentation Associations
ECMS	Electronic Copyright Management Systems
ECUF	Educational Copyright Users Forum
EEA	European Economic Area
EFPICC	European Fair Practices in Copyright Campaign
ERA	Educational Recording Agency
FAST	Federation Against Software Theft
FE	further education
FTE	full-time equivalent student: full-time students plus part-time students expressed as full-time students
HEI	higher education institution
IAML (UK)	International Association of Music Librarians (UK)
ICOLC	International Coalition of Library Consortia
IFLA	International Federation of Library Associations and Institutions
IFPI	International Federation of Phonographic Industries
ISP	internet service provider
LACA	Libraries and Archives Copyright Alliance
LEA	Local Education Authority
MCPS	Mechanical Copyright Protection Society
MLE	managed learning environment
MPA	Music Publishers Association
NBU	National Blind Union
NLA	Newspaper Licensing Agency
OCR	optical character recognition
OHP	overhead projector
OJ	Official Journal of the European Union
OSP	online service provider (American)

PLS	Publishers Licensing Society
PPL	Phonographic Performance Limited
PRS	Performing Right Society
RIAA	Recording Industry Association of America
rights holder	The one who holds the economic right or rights to the work at the time. This may be the original author, the author's heir, the publisher, producer, exclusive licensee or anyone else who has a legal right to control the copyright.
RNIB	Royal National Institute for the Blind
RNID	Royal National Institute for Deaf people
RRO	Reproductive rights organization; also called a collecting society or licensing organization or agency
SCONUL	Society of College, National and University Libraries
SCOP	Standing Conference of Principals. Represents specialist colleges in HE
TEACH	Technology, Education and Copyright Harmonization Act (USA)
time-shifting	Recording of a broadcast solely for the purpose of enabling it to be viewed or listened to at a more convenient time
TPMs	technical protection measures
TRIPS	Trade-Related aspects of Intellectual Property rights
UCAS	Universities and Colleges Admissions Service
UCC	Universal Copyright Convention
UCITA	Uniform Computer Information Transactions Act (USA)
UUK	Universities UK. The umbrella body for higher education, formerly CVCP
VLE	virtual learning environment
VLV	Voice of the Listener and Viewer
WIPO	World Intellectual Property Organization
WTO	World Trade Organization

Appendix A
Prescribed copyright declaration form for published works

To:

The Librarian of .... Library
(Address of Library)

Please supply me with a copy of:

the article in the periodical, the particulars of which are ....
or
the part of the published work, the particulars of which are ....

required by me for the purposes of research or private study.

I declare that:

a) I have not previously been supplied with a copy of the same material by you or any other librarian;
b) I will not use the copy except for research for a non-commercial purpose or private study and will not supply a copy of it to any other person; and
c) to the best of my knowledge no other person with whom I work or study has made or intends to make, at or about the same time as this request, a request for substantially the same material for substantially the same purpose.

I understand that if the declaration is false in a material particular the copy supplied to me by you will be an infringing copy and that I shall be liable for infringement of copyright as if I had made the copy myself.

Signature: ....
This must be the personal signature of the person making the request. A stamped or typewritten signature, or the signature of an agent is NOT acceptable.

Date:..

Name (please print): ....

Address:..
....
....

Appendix B
Prescribed copyright declaration form for unpublished works

To:

    The Librarian /Archivist of ....Library/Archive
    [Address of Library/Archive]

Please supply me with a copy of:

the whole/following part [particulars of part] of the [particulars of the unpublished work] required by me for the purposes of :

    research for a non-commercial purpose   [ ] *or*
    private study.   [ ]

I declare that:

a) I have not previously been supplied with a copy of the same material by you or any other librarian or archivist;
b) I will not use the copy except for non-commercial research or private study and will not supply a copy of it to any other person; and
c) to the best of my knowledge the work had not been published before the document was deposited with your library/archive and the copyright owner has not prohibited the copying of the work.

I understand that if the declaration is false in a material particular the copy supplied to me by you will be an infringing copy and that I shall be liable for infringement of copyright as if I had made the copy myself.

Signature[1]: ....

Date:...

Name (please print): ....
Address:..
....
....

[1] This must be the personal signature of the person making the request. A stamped or typewritten signature, or the signature of an agent is NOT acceptable.

Appendix C
Organization contact details

ACID (Anti Copying in Design)
www.acid.uk.com

ALCS, Marlborough Court, 14–18 Holborn, London EC1N 2LE
Tel: 020 7395 0600; alcs@alcs.co.uk; www.alcs.co.uk

ASLIB-IMI Temple Chambers, 3–7 Temple Avenue, London EC4Y 0HP
Tel: 020 7583 8900; aslib@aslib.com; www.aslib.com

Association of Learned and Professional Society Publishers, South House,
The Street, Clapham, Worthing, West Sussex BN13 3UU
Tel: 01903 871686; sec-gen@alpsp.org; www.alpsp.org

BPI, Riverside Building, County Hall, Westminster Bridge Road, London SE1
7JA
Tel: 020 7803 1300; general@bpi.co.uk; www.bpi.co.uk

British Copyright Council, Copyright House, 29-30 Berners Street, London
W1P 4AA
Tel: 020 7359 1895; british.copyright.council@dial.pipex.com

British Music Rights, British Music House, 26 Berners Street, London W1P
3DB
Tel: 020 7306 4446; britishmusic@bmr.org; http://www.bmr.org

British Standards Institution, 389 Chiswick High Road, London W4 4AL
Tel: 020 8996 9000; info@bsi.org.uk; www.bsi.org.uk

British Video Association, 167 Great Portland Street, London W1W 5PE
Tel: 020 7436 0041; www.bva.org

Chivers-Ramesis, Windsor Bridge Road, Bath BA2 3AX
www.chivers.co.uk

Christian Copyright Licensing International (CCLI), PO Box 1339,
Eastbourne, East Sussex BN21 4SA
Tel: 01323 417711; info@ccli.co.uk; www.ccli.co.uk

CILIP, 7 Ridgmount Street, London WC1E 7AE
Tel: 020 7636 7543; info@la-hq.org.uk; www.cilip.org.uk

Copyright Circle (Graham Cornish), 33 Mayfield Grove, Harrogate, North
Yorkshire HG1 5HD
Tel: 01423 529928; gp-jm.Cornish@virgin.net; www.copyrightcircle.co.uk

Copyright Licensing Agency, 90 Tottenham Court Road, London W1P 0LP
Tel: 020 7631 5555; cla@cla.co.uk; www.cla.co.uk

Design and Artists Copyright Society, Parchment House, 13 Northburgh
Street, London EC1V 0JP

Tel: 020 7336 8811; info@dacs.co.uk; www.dacs.co.uk

EBLIDA, Grote Marktstraat 43, The Hague, The Netherlands (PO Box 16359, NL-2500 BJ The Hague)
Tel: +31 70-309 0551; eblida@debibliotheken.nl; www.eblida.org

Educational Copyright Users Forum (c/o SCONUL)
102 Euston Street, London NW1 2HA
Tel: 020 7387 0317; www.sconul.ac.uk

Educational Recording Agency, New Premier House, 150 Southampton Row, London WC1B 5AL
Tel: 020 7837 3222; era@era.org.uk; www.era.org.uk

HMSO, Copyright Unit, St Clements House, 2–16 Colegate, Norwich NR3 1BQ
Tel: 01603 723001; Fax: 01603 723000; www.hmso.gov.uk/copy.htm

IFLA, PO Box 95312, 2509 CH The Hague, The Netherlands
Tel: +31 70 314 0884; www.ifla.org

International Coalition of Library Consortia (ICOLC)
www.library.yale.edu/consortia

Libraries and Archives Copyright Alliance (LACA), CILIP, 7 Ridgmount Street, London WC1E 7AE
Tel: 020 7255 0500; info@cilip.org.uk; www.cilip.org.uk/laca

Mechanical Copyright Protection Society, Copyright House, 29–33 Berners Street, London W1P 4AA
Tel: 020 7580 5544; info@mcps.co.uk; www.mcps.co.uk

Museums Copyright Group
www.mda.org.uk/mcopyg/index.htm

Music Publishers Association Ltd, 3rd Floor, Strand Gate, 18–20 York Buildings, London WC2N 6JU
Tel: 020 7839 7779; mpa@musicpublishers.co.uk; www.mpaonline.org.uk

Newspaper Licensing Agency Ltd, Lonsdale Gate, Lonsdale Gardens, Tunbridge Wells, Kent TN1 1NL
Tel: 01892 525273; copy@nla.co.uk; www.nla.co.uk

Office for Official Publications of the European Communities, 2 rue de Mercier, L2985 Luxembourg
Tel: +352 499 28 2565; Fax: +352 499 10 62 16

Open University Educational Enterprises Ltd, 12 Cofferidge Close, Stony Stratford, Milton Keynes MK11 1BY
Tel: 01908 261662; OUEEEnq@open.ac.uk

Ordnance Survey, Copyright Branch, Romsey Road, Maybush, Southampton SO9 4DH
Tel: 01703 792706; copyrightenquiries@ordsvy.gov.uk; www.ordsvy.gov.uk

The Patent Office, Copyright Directorate, Harmsworth House, 13–15 Bouverie Street, London EC4Y 8DP

Tel: 020 7596 6566; copyright@patent.gov.uk;
www.intellectual-property.gov.uk

Performing Right Society, Copyright House, 29–33 Berners Street, London
W1P 4AA
Tel: 020 7580 5544; info@prs.co.uk; www.prs.co.uk

Phonographic Performance Ltd, 1 Upper James Street, London W1F 9DE
Tel: 020 7534 1030; www.ppluk.com

Publishers Association, 29B Montague Street, London WC1B 6BH
Tel: 020 7691 9191; www.publishers.org.uk

Publishers Licensing Society, 37-41 Gower Street, London WC1E 6HH
Tel: 020 7299 7730; www.pls.org.uk

SCONUL, 102 Euston Road, London NW1 2HA
Tel: 020 7387 0317; www.sconul.ac.uk

Society of Authors, 84 Drayton Gardens, London SW10 9SB
Tel: 020 7373 6642; www.writers.org.uk/society/

TFPL, 17–18 Britton Street, London EC1M 5TL
Tel: 020 7251 5522; www.tfpl.com

UNESCO, 1 rue Miollis, 75732 Paris Cedex 15, France
Tel: +33 1 45 68 47 07; www.unesco.org

Universities UK, Woburn House, 20 Tavistock Square, London WC1H 9HQ
Tel: 020 7419 4111; www.UniversitiesUK.ac.uk

Video Performance Ltd, 1 Upper James Street, London W1F 9DE
Tel: 020 7534 1400; www.musicmall.co.uk

WIPO, 34 Chemin des Columbettes, PO Box 18, CH-1211, Geneva 20,
Switzerland.
Tel: +41 22 338 9111; COPYRIGHT.mail@wipo.int; www.wipo.int

WTO, rue de Lausanne 154, CH-1211, Geneva 21, Switzerland
Tel: +41 22 739 5111; enquiries@wto.org; www.wto.org

Index